ALSO PRODUCED BY BRIAN GRAZER

FILM

A Beautiful Mind
Frost/Nixon
8 Mile
The Da Vinci Code
The Doors
Made in America
Rush
American Gangster
Inside Man
Friday Night Lights
Dr. Seuss' How the Grinch Stole Christmas!
Apollo 13
Blue Crush
Liar Liar
The Nutty Professor
Parenthood
Splash

TELEVISION

The 84th Academy Awards
Friday Night Lights
Sports Night
Arrested Development
24
Parenthood

A CURIOUS MIND

The Secret to a Bigger Life

BRIAN GRAZER

and

CHARLES FISHMAN

Simon & Schuster

New York   London   Toronto   Sydney   New Delhi

Simon & Schuster
1230 Avenue of the Americas
New York, NY 10020

First Simon & Schuster hardcover edition April 2015

SIMON & SCHUSTER and colophon are registered trademarks of Simon & Schuster, Inc.

For information about special discounts for bulk purchases, please contact Simon & Schuster Special Sales at 1-866-506-1949 or business@simonandschuster.com.

The Simon & Schuster Speakers Bureau can bring authors to your live event. For more information or to book an event contact the Simon & Schuster Speakers Bureau at 1-866-248-3049 or visit our website at www.simonspeakers.com.

Interior design by Joy O'Meara
Jacket design by Jason Heuer
Jacket image by Jeff Koons

Manufactured in the United States of America

10 9 8 7 6 5 4 3 2 1

Library of Congress Cataloging-in-Publication Data

Grazer, Brian, 1953–
A curious mind : the secret to a bigger life / Brian Grazer, Charles Fishman.
pages cm
Summary: "From Academy Award–nominated producer Brian Grazer and acclaimed business journalist Charles Fishman comes a brilliantly entertaining peek into the weekly "curiosity conversations" that have inspired Grazer to create some of America's favorite and iconic movies and television shows—from *24* to *A Beautiful Mind*. For decades, film and TV producer Brian Grazer has scheduled a weekly "curiosity conversation" with an accomplished stranger. From scientists to spies, and adventurers to business leaders, Grazer has met with anyone willing to answer his questions for a few hours. These informal discussions sparked the creative inspiration behind many of Grazer's movies and TV shows, including *Splash, 24, A Beautiful Mind, Apollo 13, Arrested Development, 8 Mile, J. Edgar,* and many others. *A Curious Mind* is a brilliantly entertaining, fascinating, and inspiring homage to the power of inquisitiveness and the ways in which it deepens and improves us. Whether you're looking to improve your management style at work or you want to become a better romantic partner, this book—and its lessons on the power of curiosity—can change your life"—Provided by publisher.
1. Curiosity. 2. Creative thinking. 3. Self-actualization (Psychology) I. Fishman, Charles, 1961– II. Title.
BF323.C8G73 2015
153.8—dc23

2014032967

ISBN 978-1-4767-3075-2
ISBN 978-1-4767-3079-0 (ebook)

For my Grandma Sonia Schwartz.
Starting when I was a boy, she treated every question I asked as valuable.
She taught me to think of myself as curious,
a gift that has served me every day of my life.

Contents

A CURIOUS MIND

A Curious Mind and a Curious Book

"I have no special talents. I am only passionately curious."

—*Albert Einstein*[1]

IT SEEMS LIKE A GOOD idea to start a book about curiosity by asking an obvious question:

What's a guy like me doing writing a book about curiosity?

I'm a movie and TV producer. I live immersed in the most densely populated epicenter of entertainment in the world: Hollywood.

Whatever picture you have of the life of a Hollywood

movie producer, I've probably lived it. We often have ten or more movies and TV shows in production at a time, so work means meeting with actors, writers, directors, musicians. The phone calls—with agents, producers, studio heads, stars—start well before I reach the office, and often follow me home in the car. I fly to the movie sets, I screen the trailers, I go to the red-carpet premieres.

My days are hectic, they're overscheduled, they're sometimes frustrating. Usually, they're great fun. They're never dull.

But I'm not a journalist or a professor. I'm not a scientist. I don't go home at night and research psychology as a secret hobby.

I'm a Hollywood producer.

So what *am* I doing writing a book about curiosity?

Without curiosity, none of this would have happened.

More than intelligence or persistence or connections, curiosity has allowed me to live the life I wanted.

Curiosity is what gives energy and insight to everything else I do. I love show business, I love telling stories. But I loved being curious long before I loved the movie business.

For me, curiosity infuses everything with a sense of possibility. Curiosity has, quite literally, been the key to my success, and also the key to my happiness.

And yet, for all the value that curiosity has brought to my life and my work, when I look around, I don't see people talking about it, writing about it, encouraging it, and using it nearly as widely as they could.

Curiosity has been the most valuable quality, the most important resource, the central motivation of my life. I think curiosity should be as much a part of our culture, our educational system, our workplaces, as concepts like "creativity" and "innovation."

That's why I decided to write a book about curiosity. It made my life better (and still does). It can make your life better too.

. . .

I AM CALLED A movie producer—I even call myself that—but really what I am is a storyteller. A couple of years ago, I started thinking about curiosity as a value I wanted to share, a quality I wanted to inspire in other people. I thought, What I'd really like to do is sit down and tell a few stories about what curiosity has done for me.

I'd like to tell stories about how curiosity has helped me make movies. I'd like to tell stories about how curiosity has helped me be a better boss, a better friend, a better businessman, a better dinner guest.

I'd like to tell stories about the sheer joy of discovery that open-ended curiosity offers. That's the kind of joy we have as kids when we learn things just because we're curious. You can keep doing that as an adult, and it's just as much fun.

The most effective way to pass on these stories—to illustrate the power and variety of curiosity—is to write them down.

So that's what you're holding in your hand. I teamed up with journalist and author Charles Fishman, and over the course of eighteen months, we talked two or three times a week—we've had more than a hundred conversations, every one of them about curiosity.

I know very well how important curiosity has been to my life. As you'll see in the coming chapters, I long ago figured out how to be systematic about using curiosity to help me tell stories, to help me make good movies, to help me learn about parts of the world far from Hollywood. One of the things I've done for thirty-five years is sit down and have conversations with people from outside show business—"curiosity conversations" with people immersed in everything from particle physics to etiquette.

But I had never turned my curiosity on curiosity itself. So I've spent the last two years thinking about it, asking questions about it, trying to understand how it works.

In the course of exploring and unpacking it, in the course of diagramming curiosity and dissecting its anatomy, we discovered something interesting and surprising. There's a spectrum of curiosity, like there's a spectrum of colors of light. Curiosity comes in different shades and different intensities for different purposes.

The technique is the same—asking questions—regardless of the subject, but the mission, the motivation, and the tone vary. The curiosity of a detective trying to solve a murder is very different from the curiosity of an architect trying to get the floor plan right for a family's house.

The result is, admittedly, a slightly unusual book. We tell it in the first person, in the voice of Brian Grazer, because the central stories come from my life and work.

Partly, then, the book is a portrait of me. But, in fact, it's more of a working portrait of curiosity itself.

Curiosity has taken me on a lifetime of journeys. Asking questions about curiosity itself in the last two years has been fascinating.

And one thing I know about curiosity: it's democratic. Anyone, anywhere, of any age or education level, can use it. One reminder of curiosity's quiet power is that there are still countries on Earth where you have to be very careful at whom you aim your curiosity. Being curious in Russia has proven fatal; being curious in China can land you in prison.

But even if your curiosity is suppressed, you can't lose it.

It's always on, always waiting to be unleashed.

The goal of *A Curious Mind* is simple: I want to show you how valuable curiosity can be, and remind you how much fun it is. I want to show you how I use it, and how you can use it.

Life isn't about finding the answers, it's about asking the questions.

CHAPTER ONE

There Is No Cure for Curiosity

"The cure for boredom is curiosity. There is no cure for curiosity."

—*Dorothy Parker*[1]

ONE THURSDAY AFTERNOON, THE SUMMER after I graduated from the University of Southern California (USC), I was sitting in my apartment in Santa Monica with the windows open, thinking about how to get some work until I started law school at USC in the fall.

Suddenly, through the windows, I overheard two guys talking just outside. One said, "Oh my God, I had the cushiest job at

Warner Bros. I got paid for eight hours of work every day, and it was usually just an hour."

This guy got my attention. I opened the window a little more so I wouldn't miss the rest of the conversation, and I quietly closed the curtain.

The guy went on to say he had been a legal clerk. "I just quit today. My boss was a man named Peter Knecht."

I was amazed. Sounded perfect to me.

I went right to the telephone, dialed 411,[2] and asked for the main number at Warner Bros.—I still remember it, 954-6000.[3]

I called the number and asked for Peter Knecht. An assistant in his office answered, and I said to her, "I'm going to USC law school in the fall, and I'd like to meet with Mr. Knecht about the law clerk job that's open."

Knecht got on the line. "Can you be here tomorrow at 3 p.m.?" he asked.

I met with him on Friday at 3 p.m. He hired me at 3:15. And I started work at Warner Bros. the next Monday.

I didn't quite realize it at that time, but two incredible things happened that day in the summer of 1974.

First, my life had just changed forever. When I reported for work as a legal clerk that Monday, they gave me a windowless office the size of a small closet. At that moment, I had found my life's work. From that tiny office, I joined the world of show business. I never again worked at anything else.

I also realized that curiosity had saved my ass that Thursday afternoon. I've been curious as long as I can remember. As a boy, I peppered my mother and my grandmother with questions, some of which they could answer, some of which they couldn't.

By the time I was a young man, curiosity was part of the way I approached the world every day. My kind of curiosity hasn't changed much since I eavesdropped on those guys at my apartment complex. It hasn't actually changed that much since I was an antsy twelve-year-old boy.

My kind of curiosity is a little wide-eyed, and sometimes a little mischievous. Many of the best things that have happened in my life are the result of curiosity. And curiosity has occasionally gotten me in trouble.

But even when curiosity has gotten me in trouble, it has been interesting trouble.

Curiosity has never let me down. I'm never sorry I asked that next question. On the contrary, curiosity has swung wide many doors of opportunity for me. I've met amazing people, made great movies, made great friends, had some completely unexpected adventures, even fallen in love—because I'm not the least bit embarrassed to ask questions.

That first job at Warner Bros. studios in 1974 was exactly like the tiny office it came with—confining and discouraging. The assignment was simple: I was required to deliver final contract and legal documents to people with whom Warner Bros. was doing business. That's it. I was given envelopes filled with documents and the addresses where they should go, and off I went.

I was called a "legal clerk," but I was really just a glorified courier. At the time, I had an old BMW 2002—one of the boxy two-door BMW sedans that looked like it was leaning forward. Mine was a faded red-wine color, and I spent my days driving around Hollywood and Beverly Hills, delivering stacks of important papers.

I quickly identified the one really interesting thing about the job: the people to whom I was bringing the papers. These were the elite, the powerful, the glamorous of 1970s Hollywood—the writers, directors, producers, stars. There was only one problem: people like that always have assistants or secretaries, doormen or housekeepers.

If I was going to do this job, I didn't want to miss out on the only good part. I didn't want to meet housekeepers, I wanted to meet the important people. I was curious about them.

So I hit on a simple gambit. When I showed up, I would tell the intermediary—the secretary, the doorman—that I had to hand the documents directly to the person for the delivery to be "valid."

I went to ICM—the great talent agency—to deliver contracts to seventies superagent Sue Mengers,[4] who represented Barbra Streisand and Ryan O'Neal, Candice Bergen and Cher, Burt Reynolds and Ali MacGraw. How did I meet Mengers? I told the ICM receptionist, "The only way Miss Mengers can receive this is if I hand it to her personally." She sent me in without another question.

If the person to whom the documents were addressed wasn't there, I'd simply leave and come back. The guy who had unwittingly tipped me to the job was right. I had all day, but not much work to worry about.

This is how I met Lew Wasserman, the tough-guy head of MCA Studios, and his partner, Jules Stein.

It's how I met William Peter Blatty, who wrote *The Exorcist*, and also Billy Friedkin, the Oscar winner who directed it.

I handed contracts to Warren Beatty at the Beverly Wilshire Hotel.

I was just twenty-three years old, but I was curious. And I quickly learned that not only could I meet these people, I could also sit and talk to them.

I would hand over the documents with graciousness and deference, and since it was the seventies, they'd always say, "Come in! Have a drink! Have a cup of coffee!"

I would use these moments to get a sense of them, sometimes to get a bit of career advice. I never asked for a job. I never asked for anything, in fact.

Pretty quickly, I realized the movie business was a lot more interesting than law school. So I put it off—I never went; I would have made a terrible lawyer—and I kept that clerk job for a year, through the following summer.

You know what's curious: throughout that entire time, no one ever called my bluff. No one said, "Hey, kid, just leave the contract on the table and get out of here. You don't need to see Warren Beatty."

I met every single person to whom I delivered papers.

Just as curiosity had gotten me the job, it also transformed the job itself into something wonderful.

The men and women whose contracts I delivered changed my life. They showed me a whole style of storytelling I wasn't familiar with, and I began to think that maybe I was a storyteller at heart. They set the stage for me to produce movies like *Splash* and *Apollo 13*, *American Gangster*, *Friday Night Lights*, and *A Beautiful Mind*.

Something else happened during that year of being a legal clerk that was just as important. It was the year I started to actively appreciate the real power of curiosity.

If you grew up in the fifties and sixties, being curious wasn't exactly considered a virtue. In the well-ordered, obedient classrooms of the Eisenhower era, it was more like an irritant. I knew I was curious, of course, but it was a little like wearing glasses. It was something people noticed, but it didn't help me get picked for sports teams, and it didn't help with girls.

That first year at Warner Bros., I realized that curiosity was more than just a quality of my personality. It was my secret weapon. Good for getting picked for the team—it would turn out to be good for becoming captain of the team—and even good for getting the girls.

* * *

CURIOSITY SEEMS SO SIMPLE. Innocent, even.

Labrador retrievers are charmingly curious. Porpoises are

playfully, mischievously curious. A two-year-old going through the kitchen cabinets is exuberantly curious—and delighted at the noisy entertainment value of her curiosity. Every person who types a query into Google's search engine and presses ENTER is curious about *something*—and that happens 4 million times a minute, every minute of every day.[5]

But curiosity has a potent behind-the-scenes power that we mostly overlook.

Curiosity is the spark that starts a flirtation—in a bar, at a party, across the lecture hall in Economics 101. And curiosity ultimately nourishes that romance, and all our best human relationships—marriages, friendships, the bond between parents and children. The curiosity to ask a simple question—"How was your day?" or "How are you feeling?"—to listen to the answer, and to ask the next question.

Curiosity can seem simultaneously urgent and trivial. Who shot J.R.? How will *Breaking Bad* end? What are the winning numbers on the ticket for the largest Powerball jackpot in history? These questions have a kind of impatient compulsion—right up until the moment we get the answer. Once the curiosity is satisfied, the question itself deflates. *Dallas* is the perfect example: who *did* shoot J.R.? If you were alive in the 1980s, you know the question, but you may not recall the answer.[6]

There are plenty of cases where the urgency turns out to be justified, of course, and where satisfying the initial curiosity only unleashes more. The effort to decode the human genome turned into a dramatic high-stakes race between two teams of scientists. And once the genome was available, the results opened a thousand fresh pathways for scientific and medical curiosity.

The quality of many ordinary experiences often pivots on curiosity. If you're shopping for a new TV, the kind you ultimately take home and how well you like it is very much dependent on a salesperson who is curious: curious enough about the TVs to know them well; curious enough about your own needs and watching habits to figure out which TV you need.

That's a perfect example, in fact, of curiosity being camouflaged.

In an encounter like that, we'd categorize the salesperson as either "good" or "bad." A bad salesperson might aggressively try to sell us something we didn't want or understand, or would simply show us the TVs for sale, indifferently parroting the list of features on the card mounted beneath each. But the key ingredient in either case is curiosity—about the customer, and about the products.

Curiosity is hiding like that almost everywhere you look—its presence or its absence proving to be the magic ingredient in a whole range of surprising places. The key to unlocking the genetic mysteries of humanity: curiosity. The key to providing decent customer service: curiosity.

If you're at a boring business dinner, curiosity can save you.

If you're bored with your career, curiosity can rescue you.

If you're feeling uncreative or unmotivated, curiosity can be the cure.

It can help you use anger or frustration constructively.

It can give you courage.

Curiosity can add zest to your life, and it can take you way beyond zest—it can enrich your whole sense of security, confidence, and well-being.

But it doesn't do any of that alone, of course.

While Labrador retrievers are really curious, no black Lab ever decoded the genome, or got a job at Best Buy for that matter. They lose interest pretty quickly.

For it to be effective, curiosity has to be harnessed to at least two other key traits. First, the ability to pay attention to the answers to your questions—you have to actually absorb whatever it is you're being curious about. We all know people who ask really good questions, who seem engaged and energized when they're talking and asking those questions, but who zone out the moment it's time for you to answer.

The second trait is the willingness to act. Curiosity was undoubtedly the inspiration for thinking we could fly to the moon, but it didn't marshal the hundreds of thousands of people, the billions of dollars, and the determination to overcome failures and disasters along the way to making it a reality. Curiosity can inspire the original vision—of a moon mission, or of a movie, for that matter. It can replenish that inspiration when morale flags—look, that's where we're going! But at some point, on the way to the moon or the multiplex, the work gets hard, the obstacles become a thicket, the frustration piles up, and then you need determination.

I hope to accomplish three things in this book: I want to

wake you up to the value and power of curiosity; I want to show you all the ways I use it, in the hopes that that will inspire you to test it out in your daily life; and I want to start a conversation in the wider world about why such an important quality is so little valued, taught, and cultivated today.

For a trait with so much potential power, curiosity itself seems uncomplicated. Psychologists define curiosity as "wanting to know." That's it. And that definition squares with our own commonsense feeling. "Wanting to know," of course, means seeking out the information. Curiosity starts out as an impulse, an urge, but it pops out into the world as something more active, more searching: a question.

This inquisitiveness seems as intrinsic to us as hunger or thirst. A child asks a series of seemingly innocent questions: Why is the sky blue? How high up does the blue go? Where does the blue go at night? Instead of answers (most adults can't explain why the sky is blue, including me), the child might receive a dismissive, slightly patronizing reply like, "Why, aren't *you* the curious little girl . . ."[7]

To some, questions like these feel challenging, even more so if you don't know the answers. Rather than answering them, the adult simply asserts his own authority to brush them aside. Curiosity can make us adults feel a little inadequate or impatient—that's the experience of the parent who doesn't know why the sky is blue, the experience of the teacher trying to get through the day's lesson without being derailed.

The girl is left not just without answers, but also with the strong impression that asking questions—innocuous or intriguing questions—can often be regarded as impertinent.

That's hardly surprising.

No one today ever says anything bad about curiosity, directly. But if you pay attention, curiosity isn't really celebrated and cultivated, it isn't protected and encouraged. It's not just that curiosity is inconvenient. Curiosity can be dangerous. Curiosity isn't just impertinent, it's insurgent. It's revolutionary.

The child who feels free to ask why the sky is blue grows into the adult who asks more disruptive questions: Why am I the serf and you the king? Does the sun really revolve around Earth? Why are people with dark skin slaves and people with light skin their masters?

How threatening is curiosity?

All you have to do is look to the Bible to see. The first story in the Bible after the story of creation, the first story that involves people, is about curiosity. The story of Adam, Eve, the serpent, and the tree does not end well for the curious.

Adam is told explicitly by God: "You are free to eat from any tree in the garden; but you must not eat from the tree of the knowledge of good and evil, for when you eat from it you will certainly die."[8]

It is the serpent who suggests challenging God's restriction. He starts with a question himself, to Eve: Is there a tree whose fruit God has put off limits? Yes, Eve says, the tree right at the center of the garden—we can't eat its fruit, we can't even touch it, or else we'll die.

Eve knows the rules so well, she embellishes them a bit: Don't even *touch* the tree.

The serpent replies with what is surely the most heedless bravado in history—unafraid of the knowledge of good and evil, or of God. He says to Eve, "You will not certainly die. For God knows that when you eat from it your eyes will be opened, and you will be like God, knowing good and evil."[9]

The serpent is appealing directly to Eve's curiosity. You don't even know what you don't know, the serpent says. With a bite of the forbidden fruit, you will see the world in a completely different way.

Eve visits the tree, and discovers that "the fruit of the tree was good for food and pleasing to the eye, and also desirable for gaining wisdom."[10]

She plucks a piece of fruit, takes a bite, and passes it to Adam, who also takes a bite. "And the eyes of both of them were opened."[11]

Knowledge was never so easily gotten, nor in the end so hard won. To say that God was angry is an understatement. The punishment for knowing good and evil is misery for Eve and Adam, and for all the rest of us, forever: the pain of childbirth for Eve, the unceasing toil of raising their own food for Adam. And, of course, banishment from the garden.

The parable could not be blunter: curiosity causes suffering. Indeed, the story's moral is aimed directly at the audience: whatever your current misery, reader, it was caused by Adam, Eve, the serpent, and their rebellious curiosity.

So there you have it. The first story, in the foundation work of Western Civilization—the very first story!—is about curiosity, and its message is: Don't ask questions. Don't seek out knowledge on your own—leave it to the people in charge. Knowledge just leads to wretchedness.

Barbara Benedict is a professor at Trinity College in Hartford, Connecticut, and a scholar of the eighteenth century who spent years studying the attitude about curiosity during that period, as scientific inquiry sought to overtake religion as the way we understand the world.

The Adam and Eve story, she says, is a warning. "'You are a serf because God said you should be a serf. I'm a king because God said I should be a king. Don't ask any questions about that.' Stories like Adam and Eve," Benedict says, "reflect the need of cultures and civilizations to maintain the status quo. 'Things are the way they are because that's the right way.' That attitude is popular among rulers and those who control information." And it has been from the Garden of Eden to the Obama administration.

Curiosity still gets no respect. We live in an era in which, if you're willing to squint, all of human knowledge is accessible on a smartphone, but the bias against curiosity still infuses our culture.

The classroom should be a vineyard of questions, a place to cultivate them, to learn both how to ask them and how to chase down the answers. Some classrooms are. But in fact, curiosity is often treated with the same regard in school as it was in the Garden of Eden. Especially with the recent proliferation of standardized testing, questions can derail the lockstep framework of the day's lesson plan; sometimes teachers don't know the answers themselves. It's exactly the opposite of what you would hope, but authentic curiosity in a typical seventh-grade classroom isn't cultivated—because it's inconvenient and disruptive to the orderly running of the class.

The situation is little better in the offices and workplaces where most adults spend their lives. Sure, software coders or pharmaceutical researchers or university professors are encouraged to be curious because it's a big part of their jobs. But what if the typical hospital nurse or bank teller gets curious and starts questioning how things are done? Outside of some truly exceptional places like Google and IBM and Corning, curiosity is unwelcome, if not insubordinate. Good behavior—whether you're fourteen years old or forty-five—doesn't include curiosity.

Even the word "curious" itself remains strangely anti-curious. We all pretend that a curious person is a delight, of course. But when we describe an object with the adjective "curious," we mean that it's an oddity, something a little weird, something other than normal. And when someone responds to a question with the tilt of her head and the statement, "That's a curious question," she is of course saying it's not the right question to be asking.

Here's the remarkable thing. Curiosity isn't just a great tool for improving your own life and happiness, your ability to win a great job or a great spouse. It is the key to the things we say we value most in the modern world: independence, self-determination, self-government, self-improvement. Curiosity is the path to freedom itself.

The ability to ask any question embodies two things: the freedom to go chase the answer, and the ability to challenge authority, to ask, "How come you're in charge?"

Curiosity is itself a form of power, and also a form of courage.

. . .

I WAS A PUDGY boy, and I didn't grow out of it as a teenager. When I graduated from college, I had love handles. I got teased at the beach. I looked soft, with my shirt on or off.

I decided I didn't want to look the way I looked. When I was twenty-two years old, I changed my diet and developed an exercise routine—a discipline, really. I jumped rope every day, Two hundred jumps a minute, thirty minutes a day, seven days a week. Six thousand jumps a day for twelve years. Gradually my body changed, the love handles faded away.

I didn't drive myself to be buff. And I don't look like a movie star. But I also don't really look like what you might imagine a movie producer looks like. I have my own slightly offbeat style. I wear sneakers to work, I gel my hair so it stands straight up, I have a big smile.

And today, I'm still exercising four or five times a week, usually first thing in the morning, often getting up before six to make sure I have time. (I don't jump rope anymore, because I eventually ruptured both my Achilles tendons.) I'm sixty-three years old, and in the last four decades, I've never slipped back into being soft.

I took a resolution and turned it into a habit, into part of how I live each day.

I did the same thing with curiosity.

Very gradually, starting with that first law clerk's job at Warner Bros., I consciously made curiosity a part of my routine.

I already explained that first step, insisting on meeting everyone whose legal contracts I delivered. I took two things from my success with that. First, people—even famous and powerful people—are happy to talk, especially about themselves and their work; and second, it helps to have even a small pretext to talk to them.

That's what my "I have to hand these papers over in person" line was, a pretext—it worked for me, it worked for the assistants, it even worked for the people I was visiting. "Oh, he needs to see me in person, sure."

A few months after I started at Warner Bros., a senior vice president of the studio was fired. I remember watching them peel his name off the office door.

His office was spacious, it had windows, it had two secretaries, and most important, it was right next to the executive suite—what I called the "royal" offices—where the president of Warner Bros. worked, as did the chairman, and the vice chairman.

I asked my boss, Peter Knecht, if I could use that vice president's office while it was empty.

"Sure," Knecht said. "I'll arrange it."

The new office changed everything. Just like when you wear the right clothes for the occasion—when you wear a suit, you feel more confident and grown up—going to work in that real office changed my perspective. All of a sudden I felt like I had my own piece of real estate, my own franchise.

This was a great time to be in show business in Hollywood, the late sixties and seventies, and the "royal suite" was occupied by three of the most important and creative people of the era—Frank Wells, the president of Warner Bros., who went on to head Disney; Ted Ashley, who wasn't ever a household name, but who as chairman of Warner Bros. really brought energy and success back to the studio; and John Calley, the vice chairman of Warner Bros., who was a legendary producer, something of a Hollywood intellectual, a creative force, and unquestionably an eccentric character.

I was just a law clerk, but I had an office, my own secretaries, and I even had one of those old-fashioned speaker-box intercoms on my desk. Just outside my door worked three of the most powerful men in Hollywood. I had created a situation where I was in exactly the right place at exactly the right time.

I was baffled by the entertainment business, and it seemed as if even many of the people in the entertainment business were baffled by it. It was hard to understand how movies and

TV shows got made. It was definitely not a linear process. People seemed to be navigating in a fog, without instruments.

But I was fascinated and captivated by it. I became like an anthropologist entering a new world, with a new language, new rituals, new priorities. It was a completely immersive environment, and it ignited my curiosity. I was determined to study it, to understand it, to master it.

It was John Calley who really showed me what being in the entertainment business was all about, and he also showed me what it could be like. Calley was a huge figure and an important creative force in the movies in the 1960s and 1970s. Under his aegis, Warner Bros. flourished, producing movies like *The Exorcist*, *A Clockwork Orange*, *Deliverance*, *Dog Day Afternoon*, *All the President's Men*, *The Towering Inferno*, *Dirty Harry*, and *Blazing Saddles*.[12]

When I was working just down the hall from him, Calley was forty-four or forty-five years old, at the height of his power, and already a legend—intelligent, eccentric, Machiavellian. Warner Bros. in those days was making a movie a month,[13] and Calley was always thinking a hundred moves ahead. A handful of people loved him, a slightly larger group admired him, and a lot of people feared him.

I think what he found appealing about me was my innocence, my utter naïveté. I wasn't working any angles. I was so new, I didn't even know where the angles were.

Calley would say, "Grazer, come sit in my office." He'd put me on the couch, and I'd watch him work.

The whole thing was a revelation. My own father was a lawyer, a sole practitioner, and he struggled to be successful. I was headed to law school—a life of manila file folders, stacks of briefs, thick casebooks, working away at a Naugahyde-topped desk.

Calley worked out of a huge office that was beautiful and elegant. It was set up like a living room. He had no desk. He had a couple of sofas, and he worked all day sitting on the sofa.

He didn't do any writing or typing, he didn't carry piles of work home from the office each day. He talked. He sat in this elegant living room, on the couch, and talked all day.[14] In fact, the contracts I delivered were just the final act, formalizing all the talk. Sitting there on Calley's sofa, it was clear that the business part of show business was all about conversation.

And watching Calley work, I realized something: creative thoughts didn't have to follow a straight narrative line. You could pursue your interests, your passions, you could chase any quirky idea that came from some odd corner of your experience or your brain. Here was a world where good ideas had real value—and no one cared whether the idea was connected to yesterday's idea or whether it was related to the previous ten minutes of conversation. If it was an interesting idea, no one cared where it came from at all.

It was an epiphany. That's how my brain worked—lots of ideas, just not organized like the periodic table.

For years, I struggled in school. I wasn't that good at sitting quietly, tucked into a little desk, following a bell schedule and filling out worksheets. That binary way of learning—either you know the answer or you don't—didn't fit my brain and didn't appeal to me. I've always felt like ideas come from all corners of my brain, and I felt that way even as a kid.

I did well in college, but only because by then I had figured out some tricks to succeeding in that environment. But the huge classes and impersonal homework assignments didn't excite me. I didn't learn that much. I was headed to law school because I had gotten in, and because I wasn't quite sure what else to do. I did at least have some idea of what it meant to be a lawyer—although, frankly, it seemed a lot like a life sentence to yet more homework assignments, assuming I passed the bar exam.

Calley, on the other hand, was one of the hippest guys in the world. He knew movie stars, he socialized with movie stars. He was highly literate—he read all the time. He sat on his couch, with ideas and decisions winging through his office all day long without rules or rigidity.

Watching him was intoxicating. I thought, I want to live in this man's world. Who needs a life of brown accordion files? I want to work on a sofa, follow my curiosity, and make movies.[15]

Sitting there in his office, I could clearly understand that the movie business was built on ideas—a steady stream of captivating ideas, new ideas every day. And it was suddenly clear to me that curiosity was the way to uncover ideas, it was the way to spark them.

I knew I was curious—the way you might know you are funny or shy. Curiosity was a quality of my personality. But until that year, I didn't connect curiosity to success in the world. In school, for instance, I had never associated being curious with getting good grades.

But at Warner Bros., I discovered the value of curiosity—and I began what I consider my curiosity journey, following it in a systematic way.

Calley and I never talked about curiosity. But being given the big office and watching Calley in action gave me another idea, a more evolved version of my meetings with the people to whom I was delivering contracts. I realized I didn't have to meet only the people Warner Bros. happened to be doing business with that day. I could see anyone in the business I wanted to see. I could see the people who sparked my curiosity simply by calling their offices and asking for an appointment.

I developed a brief introduction for the secretaries and assistants who answered the phone: "Hi, my name is Brian Grazer. I work for Warner Bros. Business Affairs. This is not associated with studio business, and I do not want a job, but I would like to meet Mr. So-and-so for five minutes to talk to him. . . ." And I always offered a specific reason I wanted to talk to everyone.

My message was clear: I worked at a real place, I only wanted five minutes on the schedule, I did *not* want a job. And I was polite.

Just like insisting on handing over the legal documents in person, the speech worked like a charm.

I talked to producer David Picker, who was at Columbia Pictures.

Then I thought maybe I could see producer Frank Yablans, and I did.

Once I'd met Yablans, I thought, Maybe I can meet Lew Wasserman, the head of MCA. And I did.

I worked myself up the ladder. Talking to one person in the movie business suggested a half dozen more people I could talk to. Each success gave me the confidence to try for the next person. It turned out I really could talk to almost anyone in the business.

That was the start of something that changed—and continues to change—my life and my career, and which ultimately inspired this book.

I started having what I called curiosity conversations. At first, they were just inside the business. For a long time, I had a rule for myself: I had to meet one new person in the entertainment business every day.[16] But pretty quickly I realized that I could actually reach out and talk to anyone, in any business that I was curious about. It's not just showbiz people who are willing to talk about themselves and their work—everyone is.

For thirty-five years, I've been tracking down people about whom I was curious and asking if I could sit down with them for an hour. I've had as few as a dozen curiosity conversations in a year, but sometimes I've done them as often as once a week. My goal was always at least one every two weeks. Once I started doing the curiosity conversations as a practice, my only rule for myself was that the people had to be from outside the world of movies and TV.

The idea wasn't to spend more time with the kinds of people I worked with every day. I had quickly discovered that the entertainment business is incredibly insular—we tend to talk only to ourselves. It's easy to think that movies and TV are a miniature version of the world. That's not just wrong, it's a perspective that leads to mediocre movies, and also to being boring.

I was so serious about the curiosity conversations that I often spent a year or more trying to arrange a meeting with particular people. I would spend hours calling, writing letters, cajoling, befriending assistants. As I got more successful and busier, I assigned one of my staff to arrange the conversations— the *New Yorker* did a little piece on the job, which came to be known as "cultural attaché." For a while, I had someone whose only job was to arrange the conversations.[17]

The point was to follow my curiosity, and I ranged as widely as I could. I sat down with two CIA directors. With both Carl Sagan and Isaac Asimov. I met with the man who invented the most powerful weapon in history and the richest man in the world. I met with people I was scared of; I met people that I really didn't want to meet.

I never meet anyone with a movie in mind (although in recent years, it's clear that some people met with me because they thought that maybe I would do a movie about them or their work). The goal for me is to learn something.

The results have always been surprising, and the connections I've made from the curiosity conversations have cascaded through my life—and the movies we make—in the most unexpected ways. My conversation with the astronaut Jim Lovell certainly started me on the path to telling the story of *Apollo 13*. But how do we convey, in a movie, the psychology of being trapped on a crippled spaceship? It was Veronica de Negri, a Chilean activist who was tortured for months by her own government, who taught me what it's like to be forced to rely completely on oneself to survive. Veronica de Negri helped us to get *Apollo 13* right as surely as Jim Lovell did.

Over time, I discovered that I'm curious in a particular sort of way. My strongest sense of curiosity is what I call emotional curiosity: I want to understand what makes people tick; I want to see if I can connect a person's attitude and personality with their work, with their challenges and accomplishments.

I met with Jonas Salk, the scientist and physician who cured polio, a man who was a childhood hero of mine. It took me more than a year to get an audience with him. I wasn't interested in the scientific method Salk used to figure out how to develop the polio vaccine. I wanted to know what it was like to help millions of people avoid a crippling disease that shadowed the childhoods of everyone when I was growing up. And he worked in a different era. He was renowned, admired, successful—but he received no financial windfall. He cured what was then the worst disease afflicting the world, and he never made a dime from that. Can you imagine that happening today? I wanted to understand the mind-set that turns a cure like that loose in the world.

I met with Edward Teller, who created the hydrogen bomb. He was an old man when I met him, working on the antimissile "Star Wars" program for President Reagan. He was another person I had to lobby for a year in order to get an hour with him. I wanted to understand the intellect of a man who creates something like the hydrogen bomb and what his sense of morality is like.

I met with Carlos Slim, the Mexican businessman who is the richest man in the world.[18] How does the richest man in the world live every day? I wanted to know what it takes to be that kind of businessman, to be so driven and determined that you win bigger than anyone else.

The truth is that when I was meeting someone like Salk or Teller or Slim, what I hoped for was an insight, a revelation. I wanted to grasp who they were. Of course, you don't usually get that with strangers in an hour.

Salk was gracious and friendly. Teller was crabby. And Carlos Slim was unlike what I expected, not brisk or businesslike or ruthless in any way. He was very warm. Very Latino. At lunch, he ordered a lot of courses, he drank wine, it seemed like he had nowhere else he wanted to be—our lunch lasted three hours.

I've done hundreds and hundreds of curiosity meetings. It's the thing I look forward to, and often the thing I end up enjoying the most. For me, when I'm learning from someone who is right in front of me, it's better than sex. It's better than success.

I had my first real curiosity conversation outside the entertainment business when I was twenty-three years old. I had been fired from the law clerk's job at Warner Bros. (after fifteen months, they thought I was having too much fun, and delivering too few documents), and I was working for the producer Edgar Scherick (*The Taking of Pelham One Two Three*, *The Stepford Wives*), trying to become a producer myself.

I went to see F. Lee Bailey. Bailey was the most famous criminal trial attorney in the country at that point, having been the lawyer for Sam Sheppard and Patty Hearst.

I had an idea for a TV series, what I was calling *F. Lee Bailey's Casebook of American Crimes*—kind of a judicial version of *Walt Disney Presents*, using an expert to narrate the stories of these great cases.

I really wanted to talk to Bailey. He was winning a lot of important cases. How did he pick them? Does he have a moral compass? How does he communicate in the courtroom—with facts? With legal points? With the morality of the case?

I wanted to understand the distinction between a lawyer's belief system and what he or she was good at. What was Bailey's purpose in life, and how did that mesh with his talents?

When I tracked him down, he was preparing for trial in a case in Las Cruces, New Mexico. For some reason he agreed to see me, so I flew out there.

It was kind of crazy. He was staying in this tiny town, at this Western-themed road motel, a little run-down, with a kidney-shaped swimming pool. I had no idea what was going to happen. I knocked on the door, he let me in—he was alone, no assistants—and he told me to come in while he practiced his arguments.

It was ungodly hot. I hung out on the couch in his room. He seemed to be creating his case right in front of me. After a little while, he sent me to the liquor store across the street to buy him a bottle of Johnny Walker Black.

He had a drink. He was pacing back and forth in the room, getting more confident, ramping up his argument, sounding really smart. He had tons of information. I didn't really understand it, but he was testing it out on me.

Right there in the motel room, I could see that the guy was a force. Spellbinding.

I flew home thinking he would be great at hosting this TV show. In those days, before reality TV and Nancy Grace and Greta Van Susteren, we were thinking of it as a miniseries. We did a deal with Bailey, we hired a writer, but in the end it never got made.

Still, sitting there on the couch in that sticky motel room, in that small town in New Mexico, listening to Bailey build his case, I realized that there's a huge distance between the noble reasons he probably went to law school—which were still there, deeply embedded in him—and what things were like at that moment.

It was a whole new way to look at lawyers and their work.

I never made a movie about F. Lee Bailey, of course, although his life is certainly rich enough for one. I didn't even make a movie about lawyers until twenty years later, when I did

Liar Liar, with Jim Carrey, about what happens to a lawyer who is forced to tell nothing but the truth for twenty-four hours straight.

For me, the curiosity conversations are just the most obvious, the most visible example of my own curiosity. They are a kind of discipline, like the exercise routine, because you don't get to talk to busy, interesting people unless you put steady effort into persuading them to see you.

But the curiosity conversations are different from the workouts in this way: I hate exercising, I just like the results. I love the curiosity conversations, while they are happening. The results—a month or a decade later—are something I count on, but they are a bonus.

In fact, of course, all I do is talk—I talk for a living. Actually, I try to listen for a living. Being a movie and TV producer means I live a version of the life John Calley showed me forty years ago. I have meetings and phone calls and conversations all day long. For me, every one of those is in fact a curiosity conversation. I don't just use curiosity to get to meet famous people, or to find good scripts. I use curiosity to make sure movies get made—on budget, on time, and with the most powerful storytelling possible. I've discovered that even when you're in charge, you are often much more effective asking questions than giving orders.

. . .

MY FIRST REAL, FULL-FLEDGED producing job was at Paramount Studios. I had an office on the backlot in what was called the

Director's Building. I was twenty-eight years old, and I had produced a couple of successful TV movies (including the first episodes of a twenty-hour miniseries on the Ten Commandments) and Paramount gave me a deal to find and produce movies.

My office was in a corner on the third floor, with views of the walkways crisscrossing the lot. I would open the window (yes, in the 1970s and 1980s, office windows still opened) and I'd watch the powerful, famous, and glamorous walking by.

I was curious about who was on the lot and who was working with whom. This was during the time when I made myself meet someone new in show business every single day. I liked to shout down from my window at the people walking by— Howard Koch, who cowrote *Casablanca*; Michael Eisner, who would become CEO of Disney; and Barry Diller, who was CEO of Paramount and Michael Eisner's boss.

One day Brandon Tartikoff was walking by. He was the president of NBC television, in the process of reviving the network with shows like *Hill Street Blues* and *Cheers* and *Miami Vice*. At thirty-two, he was already one of the most powerful people in show business.

"Hey Brandon!" I yelled. "Up here!"

He looked up at me and smiled. "Wow," he said, "you must be in charge of the world from up there."

A few minutes later, my phone rang. It was my boss, Gary Nardino, the head of TV at Paramount. "Brian, what the fuck do you think you're doing, screaming out your window at the president of NBC?"

"I'm just connecting," I said. "We're just having fun."

"I don't think we're having that much fun," Nardino said. "Cut it out."

Okay, not everyone was equally charmed by my style in those days. I was a little scared of Nardino, but not scared enough to stop shouting out the window.

One day I saw Ron Howard walking by. Ron was already famous and successful from his years acting on *The Andy Griffith Show* and *Happy Days*, but he was trying to make the leap to directing. As he was walking by, I thought, I'm going to meet Ron Howard tomorrow.

I didn't shout out the window at him. I waited until he got back to his office and called him up. "Ron, it's Brian Grazer," I said. "I see you on the lot. I'm a producer here too. I think we have similar goals. Let's meet and talk about it."

Ron was kind of shy, and he seemed surprised by my phone call. I don't think he really wanted to meet me. I said, "It'll be fun, it'll be relaxed, let's just do it."

A few days later, he did come by to talk. He was trying to become a mainstream movie director, and I was trying to become a mainstream movie producer. We were two guys trying to do something we'd never done before.

The moment he walked into my office, he had this aura about him—a glow. After talking to him, I could tell my choices in life weren't as thoughtful as his. He gave this sense of having a strong moral conscience. I know that sounds silly after just a single meeting, but it was my immediate impression. And it's true. It's the way Ron is today—and it's the way he was thirty-five years ago.

When he walked in, I asked him, "What do you want to be?"

Ron not only wanted to direct, he wanted to direct an R-rated movie. He wanted to change the way people saw him. I had no idea if he could direct. But I immediately decided I was going to bet on him, and try to persuade him to work with me. I started pitching my movie ideas—*Splash* and *Night Shift*. He definitely didn't want to do a movie about a man falling in love with a mermaid. But he liked the irreverence of *Night Shift*, an R-rated comedy about two guys who run a call-girl ring out of the New York City morgue. Not the movie you'd ever predict from the star of *Happy Days*.

In fact, we made two movies together—*Night Shift*, and then, despite Ron's initial reluctance, *Splash*, which became a huge hit. After working so well together on those two movies, we formed our company, Imagine Entertainment, and we've been artistic and business partners for the last thirty years. Not only could Ron direct, he's become a master filmmaker. The movies we've done together include *Parenthood, Backdraft, The Da Vinci Code, Frost/Nixon, Apollo 13*, and the Oscar-winning *A Beautiful Mind*.

My relationship with Ron has been the most important in my life, outside of my family. He's my closest work colleague, and my best friend. I decided to meet Ron after seeing him from my window, and it was my emotional curiosity—my puzzling over what makes Ron Howard *Ron Howard*—that connected me to him. Again, at one of the most important moments of my life, following my curiosity opened the door.

Ron and I are different in many ways—especially our temperaments. But we share a sense of standards, including how to tell a story, and most important, we agree on what makes a great story. In fact, if there's anyone I know who is as genuinely curious as I am, it's Ron Howard. When we're in meetings together, he asks as many questions as I do, and his questions are different, and they elicit different information.

My curiosity conversations are something I've done with consistency and purpose for thirty-five years. You'll see many examples of them throughout this book. These conversations are events or occasions when curiosity itself is the motivation.

But in my everyday work and life, curiosity itself is not an "occasion." It's the opposite. Curiosity is something I use all the time. I'm always asking questions. For me, it's an instinct. It's also, very distinctly, a technique.

I'm a boss—Ron Howard and I run Imagine together—but I'm not much of an order giver. My management style is to ask questions. If someone's doing something I don't understand, or don't like, if someone who works for me is doing something unexpected, I start out asking questions. Being curious.

I'm constantly meeting new people—sometimes at events, but often the new people are sitting on the couch in my office during the workday. I'm not particularly outgoing, but I have to *act* outgoing all the time. So how do I handle all these new people—sometimes a dozen in a single day—often sitting eagerly right in front of me, expecting me to run the conversation? I ask questions, of course. I let them do the talking. Being interested in someone isn't that hard if you know even a little about them—and as I've discovered, people love talking about their work, what they know about, their journey.

The entertainment business requires a huge amount of confidence. You have to believe in your own ideas for movies and TV shows, and you quickly discover that the safest answer for any studio or investor or executive to give is "no." I'm often amazed that we get any movies made at all. But you can't succeed in Hollywood if you're discouraged by being told "no," because regardless of the actual quality of your ideas, or even the quality of your track record, you'll get told "no" all the time. You have to have the confidence to push forward. That's true in all corners of the world—you have to have confidence if you work at a Silicon Valley tech company or treat patients at an inner-city hospital. My confidence comes from curiosity. Yes, asking questions builds confidence in your own ideas.

Curiosity does something else for me: it helps me cut through the routine anxiety of work and life.

I worry, for instance, about becoming complacent—I worry that out here in Hollywood, I'll end up in a bubble isolated from what's going on in the rest of the world, from how it's changing and evolving. I use curiosity to pop the bubble, to keep complacency at bay.

I also worry about much more ordinary things—I worry about giving speeches; I worry about the safety of my kids; I even worry about the police—police officers make me nervous. I use curiosity when I'm worried about something. If you understand what kind of speech someone wants you to give, if you understand how cops think, you'll either see your fear dissipate, or you'll be able to handle it.

I use curiosity as a management tool.

I use it to help me be outgoing.

I use curiosity to power my self-confidence.

I use it to avoid getting into a rut, and I use it to manage my own worries.

In the coming chapters, I'm going to analyze and tell stories about these different types of curiosity, because I think they can be useful to almost anyone.

And that is the most important way I use curiosity: I use it to tell stories. That, really, is my profession. My job as a producer is to look for good stories to tell, and I need people to write those stories, to act in them, to direct them. I'm looking for the money to get those stories made, and for ideas about how to sell the finished stories to the public. But, for me, the key to all these elements is the story itself.

Here's one of the secrets of life in Hollywood—a secret you learn in ninth-grade English class, but that many people forget. There are only a few kinds of stories in the world: romance, quest, tragedy, comedy. We've been telling stories for 4,000 years. Every story has been told.

And yet here I sit in the middle of a business devoted to either finding new stories, or taking old stories and telling them in fresh ways, with fresh characters.

Good storytelling requires creativity and originality; it requires a real spark of inspiration. Where does the spark come from? I think curiosity is the flint from which flies the spark of inspiration.

In fact, storytelling and curiosity are natural allies. Curiosity is what drives human beings out into the world every day, to ask questions about what's going on around them, about people and why they behave the way they do. Storytelling is the act of bringing home the discoveries learned from curiosity. The story is a report from the front lines of curiosity.

Storytelling gives us the ability to tell everyone else what we've learned—or to tell everyone the story of our adventure, or about the adventures of the people we've met. Likewise, nothing sparks curiosity like good storytelling. Curiosity drives the desire to keep reading the book you can't put down, it's the desire to know how much of a movie you've just seen is true.

Curiosity and storytelling are intertwined. They give each other power.

What makes a story fresh is the point of view of the person telling it.

I produced a movie called *Splash*, about what happens when a man falls in love with a mermaid.

I produced a movie called *Apollo 13*, the true story of what happens when three U.S. astronauts get trapped in their crippled spaceship.

I produced a movie called *8 Mile*, about trying to be a white rap musician in the black rap world of Detroit.

I produced a movie called *American Gangster*, about a heroin smuggler in Vietnam-era New York.

American Gangster isn't about a gangster—it's about capability, it's about talent and determination.

8 Mile isn't about rap music, it isn't even about race—it's about surmounting humiliation, about respect, about being an outsider.

Apollo 13 isn't about aeronautics—it's about resourcefulness, about putting aside panic in the name of survival.

And *Splash*, of course, isn't about mermaids—only a thousand people in Hollywood told me we couldn't make a movie about mermaids. *Splash* is about love, about finding the right love for yourself, as opposed to the love others would choose for you.

I don't want to make movies about alluring mermaids or courageous astronauts, about brazen drug smugglers or struggling musicians. At least, I don't want to make predictable movies about *only* those things.

I don't want to tell stories where the "excitement" comes from explosions or special effects or sex scenes.

I want to tell the very best stories I can, stories that are memorable, that resonate, that make the audience think, that sometimes make people see their own lives differently. And to find those stories, to get to inspiration, to find that spark of creativity, what I do is ask questions.

What kind of story is it? Is it a comedy? A myth? An adventure?

What's the right tone for this story?

Why are the characters in this story in trouble?

What connects the characters in this story to each other?

What makes this story emotionally satisfying?

Who is telling this story, and what is that person's point of view? What is his challenge? What is her dream?

And most important, what is this story about? The plot is what happens in the story, but that plot is not what the story is *about*.

I don't think I'd be very good at my job if I weren't curious. I think I'd be making movies that weren't very good.

I keep asking questions until something interesting happens. My talent is to know enough to ask the questions, and to know when something interesting happens.

What I think is so exciting about curiosity is that it doesn't matter who you are, it doesn't matter what your job is, or what your passion is. Curiosity works the same way for all of us—if we use it well.

You don't have to be Thomas Edison. You don't have to be Steve Jobs. You don't have to be Steven Spielberg. But you can be "creative" and "innovative" and "compelling" and "original"— because you can be curious.

Curiosity doesn't only help you solve problems—no matter

what those problems are. There's a bonus: curiosity is free. You don't need a training course. You don't need special equipment or expensive clothing, you don't need a smartphone or a high-speed Internet connection, you don't need the full set of the *Encyclopædia Britannica* (which I was always a little sad I didn't have).

You're born curious, and no matter how much battering your curiosity has taken, it's standing by, ready to be awakened.

CHAPTER TWO

The Police Chief, the Movie Mogul, and the Father of the H-Bomb: Thinking Like Other People

"Curiosity . . . is insubordination in its purest form."

—*Vladimir Nabokov*[1]

THE POLICE OFFICERS ASKED ME to lower my pants. That's when I wondered what I had gotten myself into.

It was April 30, 1992, and I was standing inside Parker Center, the distinctive downtown LA building that was then headquarters for the Los Angeles Police Department. I had been working for months to get to this spot—to meet Daryl Gates, the legendary chief of the LAPD, a man renowned for inventing the modern police SWAT unit, and for showing big-city police departments across the country how to function more like paramilitary units.

In Los Angeles in the 1980s and early 1990s, no one wielded power like Chief Gates. I was fascinated by that power, and by the personality that was able to accumulate it and use it. This type of influence is completely alien to me. I don't see the world as a hierarchy—as a chain of command. I don't want control over hundreds of people, I don't see life, or work, as an opportunity to build up power and exercise it. I don't particularly like giving orders, or seeing whether people have enough respect for me, or fear of me, to obey those orders. But the world is filled with people maneuvering for power—in fact, the typical workplace is filled with people like that, and we probably need them.

As much as I'm fascinated by that kind of power, I'm also wary of it. I do want to understand that kind of personality, as a storyteller and also as a citizen. Chief Gates made a great curiosity conversation—the perfect example of a certain kind of autocratic mind-set, right in my own city.

I tried for many months to get on Gates's calendar— working my way through an assistant, a secretary, one cop, another cop. Finally, in early 1992, his office gave me an appointment to have lunch with Chief Gates—four months into the future.

And then, on April 29, 1992, the day before my lunch, the

four LA police officers who had been caught on videotape beating Rodney King were acquitted of the charges against them, and rioting started across Los Angeles.

I got up that Thursday morning—April 30—and the rioting had gone on all night, with buildings being burned and neighborhoods being looted. Suddenly, it was the most chaotic moment in Los Angeles in thirty years, since the Watts riots in 1965. The Los Angeles Police Department was at the center of the chaos—it was the reason for it, and also responsible for stopping it. Chief Gates completely embodied the militaristic approach that led to the Rodney King beating in the first place.

I thought for sure Gates would have enough to handle that morning and that our lunch would certainly be canceled. But no—lunch was a go.

When I got to Parker Center, it was locked down. There were concrete barriers out front, and a line of police officers, and a series of checkpoints to get into the building. They asked, "Who are you going to see?" And I answered, "Chief Daryl Gates."

I produced my ID. In the lobby there was another line of cops. A couple of them patted me down. They asked me to lower my pants. Being searched to my underwear by two uniformed LAPD officers did nothing to reduce my wariness of the police, but I wanted to see Daryl Gates; I'd been trying to see him for more than a year. With my pants pulled back up, I was escorted onto the elevator by a pair of officers who rode up to the sixth floor with me.

Parker Center vibrated with energy. Although the building

was populated by the people we rely on to be cool in a crisis, it felt like everyone was a little freaked out.

I arrived at Chief Gates's suite—an outer room and his office. Everyone around me was in uniform, including the chief. He was sitting at an ordinary, utilitarian conference table in his office, surrounded by wooden chairs resembling schoolroom chairs, with arms. He was seated on one side, and I took a seat at the end.

Chief Gates seemed totally relaxed. Downstairs, the city was burning, exploding. That very afternoon, the mayor would impose a state of emergency and a curfew and call out the National Guard; the next night, President George H. W. Bush would give a televised, prime-time speech to the nation about the LA riots.[2]

But Daryl Gates was calm.

He greeted me. "What would you like for lunch?" he asked. I was so nervous, I didn't quite know what to say. "What are you having, sir?" I asked.

"I'm having a tuna sandwich," Gates said.

"I'll have what you're having." A few minutes later, an aide delivered two tuna sandwiches with potato chips on the side.

We chatted while eating our tuna and chips. Or Chief Gates was eating, at least. I couldn't take more than a few polite bites of my sandwich.

As we sat there, Gates's chief lieutenant suddenly burst into the office, totally adrenalized, shouting, "Boss! Boss! You're on TV again right now, the city council says you're out, they say they are firing you!"

Gates turned to me. He didn't flinch. Nothing in his bio-chemistry changed at all. He appeared totally calm.

He said, to me and to his lieutenant, "No chance. I'll be here as long as I want to be. They'll never get me out."

He said it in a totally matter-of-fact way, just as he might ask, "How's that tuna sandwich?"

His ego, his arrogance, was just completely imperturbable. He had been in intense situations all his life. He wasn't act-ing—for him, it was the sum total of seconds, minutes, hours, days, months of working under incredible pressure, and mas-tering it.

He had accumulated all this authority, the ability and the willingness to use it. He was totally acclimated to it. He had become unflappable, impervious to the possibility that any-thing outside his own will could change his life.

In fact, the city council had announced his replacement just two weeks before the Rodney King riots broke out. Gates had been vague about when he would leave—and got more stub-born after the riots. His cool cockiness with me notwithstand-ing, six weeks after our lunch he formally announced his resignation, and he was gone as chief two weeks after that.[3]

My visit with Daryl Gates was strange, memorable, unset-tling. In other words, it was perfect.

Some people might have been curious why Gates became a police officer, and how he climbed the ladder to become chief of an 8,000-officer force.[4] Some people might have been curi-ous how a man like Gates spent his workday—what did he pay attention to, in terms of what was going on in the city? Some people might have wondered what being immersed in nothing but the crimes of Los Angeles does to one's view of such a beautiful city, and to the view of its people.

My mission was different. I wanted a sense of the personality of someone who wears the chief's uniform with absolute confidence, who commands a miniature paramilitary state.

What does an encounter like that do for me?

First, it gets me completely out of the world I live in. For a few hours, I lived in Daryl Gates's universe—a world that could not be more different from my own. From the moment he opened his eyes in the morning to the moment he closed his eyes at night, every single day, it's likely that Chief Gates dealt with things that I had probably never even considered.

The big stuff is different—his goals, his priorities, his values.

The minutiae are different—how he dresses, how he carries himself, how he talks to the people around him.

Daryl Gates and I lived in the same city, we were both in positions of influence, we were both successful, but our worlds were so different, they hardly overlapped. We literally looked at the very same city from completely different perspectives, every day.

That's what Daryl Gates did for me: he completely disrupted my point of view.

• • •

WE ARE ALL TRAPPED in our own way of thinking, trapped in our own way of relating to people. We get so used to seeing the world our way that we come to think that the world *is* the way we see it.

For someone who makes his living finding and telling stories on movie and TV screens, that parochialism can be dangerous. It's also boring.

One of the most important ways I use curiosity every day is to see the world through other people's eyes, to see the world in ways I might otherwise miss. It's totally refreshing to be reminded, over and over, how different the world looks to other people. If we're going to tell stories that are compelling and also varied, we need to be able to capture those points of view.

Consider for a moment just a few of the seventeen movies that Ron Howard and I have made together, that I've produced and Ron has directed.

There's *Night Shift*, with Michael Keaton running a callgirl ring out of the New York City morgue, and *Parenthood*, about Steve Martin's effort to juggle work and being a good father.

There's *Backdraft*, about the courage firefighters require and the split-second judgment they need on the job, and *A Beautiful Mind*, the story of John Nash, who was both a Nobel Prize–winning mathematician and a schizophrenic.

There's *How the Grinch Stole Christmas!* with Jim Carrey bringing Dr. Seuss's Grinch to life, and *Frost/Nixon*, the drama behind David Frost's television interviews with ex-president Richard Nixon.

Those six movies capture the perspective of a raffish morgue attendant, a funny but self-critical father, a team of fearless firefighters, a brilliant but mentally ill mathematician, a cartoon misanthrope, and a canny TV journalist interviewing a disgraced former president.

That's a wonderfully varied range of characters, a wild array of points of view, stories that include comedy and quest and tragedy, settings that range from Princeton University during the Cold War to the inside of a burning skyscraper in the eighties, from the cold room at the New York City morgue to suburban America. They don't seem to have anything in common—and yet they not only came from the same company, Imagine, but all of them were shepherded by Ron and me.

That's the kind of work I want to do, and have always wanted to do, in Hollywood. I don't want to produce the same movie over and over again with slightly different characters—even unconsciously.[5]

So how does this relate to my conversation with LAPD Chief Daryl Gates?

Curiosity. I don't know how other people in the story business keep themselves from going stale, but my secret is curiosity—and specifically the curiosity conversations.

The variety in my work (and my life) comes from curiosity. It is the tool I use to search out different kinds of characters and stories than I would be able to make up on my own. Some people can dream up a person like Daryl Gates. I have to meet someone like that in person. To see how the world looks from his perspective, I have to sit in the same room with him. I have to ask him questions for myself and not only hear how he answers, but see how the expression on his face changes as he answers.

The curiosity conversations have a critical rule, an almost completely counterintuitive rule: I never have a curiosity conversation in order to find a movie to make. I have the conversations because I'm interested in a topic or a person. The conversations have allowed me to build up a reservoir of experiences and points of view.

Often, in fact, what happens is not that a conversation will inspire a movie or an idea—just the opposite. Someone will develop an idea for a movie or TV show—someone at Imagine will have an inspiration, a writer or a director will come to us with a story, I'll have an idea—and a curiosity conversation I've had years earlier will bring all the possibilities of that idea to life for me.

The richness and variety of four decades of movies and TV shows have depended on the curiosity conversations, but these meetings don't create the movies and TV shows in the first place. Curiosity spurs me to chase my passions. It also keeps me plugged in to what's going on in science, in music, in popular culture. It's not just what's happening that's important; it's the attitude, the mood that surrounds what's happening.

In 2002, when I produced the movie *8 Mile*, about hip-hop music in Detroit, I was fifty-one years old. The movie had its spark when I saw Eminem perform one night on the Video Music Awards (the VMAs). I'd been paying attention to hip-hop musicians for two decades—I'd wanted to do a movie about the hip-hop world since the 1980s, when I met Chuck

D from Public Enemy, Slick Rick, the Beastie Boys, and Russell Simmons, who founded the hip-hop label Def Jam. The idea for *8 Mile* crystallized when music producer Jimmy Iovine brought Eminem to the office, and the three of us sat down to talk about what a hip-hop movie might look like. Eminem actually spent the first forty minutes not talking. Finally I said to him, "C'mon! Talk! Animate!" And he gave me one final glare, and then he told his life story, the harrowing tale of his upbringing in Detroit. That became the spine of the movie.

About the farthest thing you can get from the tumultuous, energetic, angry, antiestablishment perspective of rap music is the buttoned-down, perfectly compartmentalized, analytical world of covert intelligence. Just as *8 Mile* was being filmed, we were also launching the TV series *24*, with Kiefer Sutherland playing counterterrorism agent Jack Bauer, whose job is to foil terrorist attacks against the United States. The first season of *24* was already in production when the real terrorist attacks of September 11, 2001, hit the United States. (The premiere of the first episode was delayed a month out of sensitivity in the aftermath of the attacks.) I loved the idea of *24*, and I connected with the sense of immediacy and urgency we tried to create in the show by unfurling it each week in real time, with an hour of the show being an hour in Jack Bauer's life.

I was ready for a show like *24*—I've been absolutely captured by the world of intelligence and covert operations for decades. I've had curiosity conversations with two CIA directors (William Colby and Bill Casey), with agents from the Israeli intelligence agency Mossad, the British intelligence agencies MI5 and MI6, and with a guy named Michael Scheuer, a former CIA operative who in 1996 helped set up and ran Alec Station, the secret CIA unit charged with tracking down Osama bin Laden before the 9/11 attacks.[6]

I'm amazed at the amount of information that people in intelligence—people at the top like Colby and Casey, and also people on the front lines like Scheuer—can accumulate and keep in their brains. They know a huge amount about how the world *really* works, and theirs is a hidden world. They know about events and relationships that are secret from the rest of us, they make decisions based on those secrets, often life-and-death decisions.

So I had years of being curious about the intelligence world, and trying to understand the motivations of those involved, and their psychology, when the TV show *24* came along. I knew a lot about the world, and I knew it could be the setting for a compelling story.

That's the long-term benefit of the conversations: the things I'm curious about create a network of information and contacts and relationships for me (not unlike the networks of information intelligence officers map out). Then when the right story comes along, it resonates with me immediately. Curiosity meant I was open to Jack Bauer in *24*, and also to the antithesis of Jack Bauer, Eminem's character in *8 Mile*, the young rapper Jimmy "B-Rabbitt" Smith.

And after that conversation I had with Daryl Gates on April 30, 1992, as our city started to riot and burn—I recognized that personality again immediately when I got the chance to produce *J. Edgar*, the movie directed by Clint Eastwood about the career of FBI director J. Edgar Hoover. Leonardo DiCaprio played Hoover. Had I not spent time trying to understand Gates twenty years earlier, I'm not sure I would have fully grasped the reality of Hoover's controlling paranoia, which Eastwood and DiCaprio infused so well into the mood, the acting, even the lighting of *J. Edgar*.

It was, in fact, one of my earliest conversations that taught me in unforgettable terms that I needed to bring ideas to the table in order to make movies—a conversation from back at Warner Bros., when I was trying to meet at least one new person each day inside show business.

I had been at Warner Bros. about a year as a legal clerk when I managed to talk my way into that meeting with Lew Wasserman. In terms of meetings, that was a stunning accomplishment—as big a deal for me at twenty-three as Jonas Salk and Edward Teller would be decades later, maybe bigger. Wasserman was the head of MCA, and he was critical in creating the modern movie business, including the idea of what we now think of as the event movie, the blockbuster. When I went to talk to him, in 1975, he had been at MCA since 1936. While he ran MCA, Wasserman had under contract movie greats like Bette Davis, Jimmy Stewart, Judy Garland, Henry Fonda, Fred Astaire, Ginger Rogers, Gregory Peck, Gene Kelly, Alfred

Hitchcock, and Jack Benny.[7] MCA's Universal Pictures had produced *Jaws* and would go on to produce *E.T. the Extra-Terrestrial, Back to the Future,* and *Jurassic Park.*

On the day I went to see him, Lew Wasserman was undoubtedly the most powerful person in the movie business. I was undoubtedly the least powerful person. It had taken me months of patient cultivation to get onto Wasserman's calendar, even for just ten minutes. I talked to his assistant Melody on a regular basis. At one point I said to her, "How about if I just come by and meet you?" And I did—just to put my face and personality with my voice.

When I finally got to see Wasserman, I wasn't nervous or particularly intimidated. I was excited. For me, it was an opportunity to get some wisdom from a man who, in fact, started out in the movie business one notch lower than me—as an usher in a movie theater. He had practically *invented* the movie business. Surely I could learn something from him.

That day, Wasserman listened without much patience to me talk about my determination to become a movie producer. He cut me short.

"Look buddy," Wasserman said, "you somehow found your way into this office. You're basically full of it. I can see that. If there are a dozen ways to become a producer—having money, knowing people who have money, having connections, having friends in the business, representing movie stars or writers—if there are a dozen ways to become a producer, you don't have any of them.

"You can't buy anything—you can't buy a script treatment. You can't buy a book. You don't know anybody. You certainly don't represent anybody. You have no leverage. You really have nothing.

"But the only way you can be anything in this business is if you own the material. You have to *own* it."

Then Wasserman reached over and grabbed a legal pad and a pencil from his desk. He slapped the pencil on the pad and handed them to me.

"Here's a yellow legal pad," he said. "Here's a number-two pencil. Put the pencil to the pad. Go write something. You have to bring the idea. Because you've got nothing else."

I was stunned, but also amazed. Wasserman was the first person to cut through the swirl of the movie business for me and say, Here's what you, Brian Grazer, can do to become a movie producer, to rise above legal clerk.

Write.

Otherwise you're all talk.

I was with Wasserman no more than ten minutes, but it felt like an hour. That time with him changed my whole perspective on the movie business—it disrupted my very youthful point of view.

What Wasserman was telling me was that since ideas were the currency in Hollywood, I had to get myself some ideas. And he was saying that since I didn't have any influence or money, I had to rely on my own curiosity and imagination as the source of those ideas. My curiosity was worth more than money—because I didn't have any money.

I didn't walk off with Wasserman's yellow legal pad and pencil. I'm pretty sure I got nervous and set them back down in his office. But I did just what he suggested: I got busy using my curiosity to create ideas.

．　．　．

WHAT DOES IT MEAN to be a great supermodel like Kate Moss, and how is that different from what it takes to be a great attorney like Gloria Allred?

If we're going to make movies that feel authentic, we have to be able to understand many corners of the world—places that operate much differently than Hollywood. As I've tried to show, I consciously use curiosity to disrupt my own point of view. I seek out people from other industries and other communities—physics, medicine, modeling, business, literature, law—and then I try to learn something about the skill and the personality it takes to perform in those worlds.

But if disrupting the point of view of someone like me—a moviemaker, a storyteller—is useful, consider how powerful it is for people doing other kinds of work.

You certainly want your doctor to be able to look at the world through your eyes—you want her to understand your symptoms, so she can give you what you need to feel better. You also want a doctor to be curious about new approaches to disease, and to care and healing. You want someone who is willing to listen to colleagues and researchers with views that may disrupt her comfortable, routine ways of taking care of patients. Medicine is full of disruptions that changed the typical ways doctors practiced it, starting with hand-washing and sanitation and coming all the way forward to laparoscopic and robotic surgery, saving or dramatically improving the lives of millions of people. Medicine is one of those arenas that steadily, sometimes radically, advances precisely because of curiosity, but you need a doctor willing to step outside her comfortable point of view in order to benefit from those improvements yourself.

Being able to imagine the perspective of others is also a critical strategic tool for managing reality in a whole range of professions. We want our police detectives to be able to imagine what criminals will do next, we want our military commanders to be able to think five moves ahead of opposing armies, we want our basketball coaches to discern the game plans of their rivals and counter them. You can't negotiate an international trade agreement without being able to understand what other nations need.

In fact, the very best doctors, detectives, generals, coaches, and diplomats all share the skill of being able to think about the world from the perspective of their rivals. You can't simply design your own strategy, then execute it and wait to see what happens so you can respond. You have to anticipate what's going to happen—by first disrupting your own point of view.

The same skill, in a completely different context, is what creates products that delight us. The specific genius of Steve Jobs lay in designing a computer operating system, and a music player, and a phone that anticipate how we'll want to compute, and listen to music, and communicate—and providing what we want before we know it. The same is true of an easy-to-use dishwasher or TV remote control.

You can always tell when you settle into the driver's seat of a car you haven't driven before whether the people who designed the dashboard and controls were the least bit curious about how their customers use their cars. The indispensable cup holder wasn't created by the engineers of great Eurocars— BMW, Mercedes, Audi. The first car cup holders debuted when Dodge launched its Caravan in 1983.[8]

With the iPhone, the cup holder, the easy-to-use dishwasher, the engineer has done something simple but often overlooked: he or she has asked questions. Who is going to use this product? What's going to be happening while they are using it? How is that person different from me?

Successful business people imagine themselves in their customers' shoes. Like coaches or generals, they also imagine what their rivals are up to, so they can be ready for the competition.

Some of this disruptive curiosity relies on instinct. Steve Jobs was famously disdainful of focus groups and consumer testing, preferring to refine products based on his own judgment.

Some of this disruptive curiosity relies on routine. During all the decades he ran Wal-Mart—the largest company in the world—founder Sam Walton convened his top five hundred managers in a meeting every Saturday morning. The "Saturday

Morning Meeting," as it was called, had just two purposes: to review in detail the week's sales, aisle-by-aisle through the store; and to ask the question: what is the competition doing that we should be paying attention to—or imitating? At every Saturday morning meeting, Walton asked his employees to stand up and talk about their visits, during the workweek, to competitors' stores—to K-mart, Zayre, Walgreens, Rite Aid, and Sears.

Walton had strict rules for this part of the meeting: participants were only allowed to talk about what competitors were doing right. They were only allowed to discuss things they'd seen that were smart and well executed. Walton was basically curious about why customers would want to shop anywhere besides Wal-Mart. He didn't care what his competitors were doing *wrong*—that couldn't hurt him. But he didn't want them to get more than a week's advantage on doing something innovative—and he knew he wasn't smart enough, alone, to imagine every possible way of running a store. Why try to guess your way into your competitors' heads when you could simply walk into their stores?

Some of this disruptive curiosity relies on systematic analysis that evolves into elaborate corporate research and development programs. It took H. J. Heinz almost three years to create the upside-down ketchup bottle—but the project got started when Heinz researchers followed consumers home and discovered they were storing their tall, thin, glass ketchup bottles precariously, upside down in their refrigerator doors, in an effort to get out the last servings of ketchup. The inverted ketchup bottle that Heinz invented as a result relies on an innovative silicone valve that seals the ketchup in, releases instantly when the bottle is squeezed, then closes immediately again when the squeezing stops. The man who invented that valve is a Michigan engineer named Paul Brown, who told a reporter, "I would pretend I was silicone and, if I was injected into a mold, what I would do." H. J. Heinz was so determined to understand its customers, it followed them home from the grocery store. Engineer Paul Brown was so determined to solve a problem, he imagined himself as liquid silicone.[9]

Procter & Gamble, the consumer products company behind Tide, Bounty, Pampers, CoverGirl, Charmin, and Crest, spends more than $1 million a day just on consumer research. P&G is so determined to understand how we clean our clothes, our kitchens, our hair, and our teeth that company researchers do 20,000 studies a year, of 5 million consumers, where the goal is principally to understand our behavior and habits. That's why Tide laundry detergent now comes in little premeasured capsules—no pouring, no measuring, no muss. That's why you can buy a Tide pen that will remove stains from your pants or your skirt, while you're wearing them.[10]

My approach to curiosity is a blend of the approaches we see in Steve Jobs, Sam Walton, and Procter & Gamble. I am, in fact, curious by instinct—I'm curious all the time. If someone walks into my office to talk about the music for a movie or about the revisions to a TV script, and that person is wearing really cool shoes, we'll start out talking about shoes.

I know that not everyone feels like they are naturally curious—or bold enough to ask about someone's shoes. But here's the secret: that doesn't matter. You can use curiosity even if you don't think of yourself as instinctively curious.

As soon as I realized the power of curiosity to make my work life better, I consciously worked on making curiosity part of my routine. I turned it into a discipline. And then I made it a habit.

But here's an important distinction between me and even the hyper-analytical folks at Procter & Gamble. I actually use the word "curiosity" to talk about what I do, to describe it, and understand it. The rest of the world, though, almost never talks about this kind of inquiry using the word "curiosity."

Even when we're being intently curious, in an organized, purposeful fashion, we don't call it "curiosity." The coach and his assistants who spend five days watching film to prepare for a game aren't considered "curious" about their opponent, even as they immerse themselves in the thinking, personality, and strategy of that team. Sports teams simply call it "watching film." Political campaigns call their form of curiosity "opposition research." Companies that spend enormous sums of money and expend enormous effort to understand their customers' behavior and satisfy their needs aren't "curious" about their customers. They use phrases like "consumer research" or say they've developed an "innovation process." (If they've hired expensive consultants to help them be curious, they say they've developed a "strategic innovation process roadmap.")

In 2011, *Harvard Business Review* published a nine-page case study of Procter & Gamble's innovation and creativity efforts. The story is coauthored by P&G's chief technology officer, and it is literally as long as this chapter, to this point—5,000 words. The authors say they want to describe P&G's effort to "systematize the serendipity that so often sparks new-business creation." In Hollywood, we call that "lunch." But "systematizing serendipity"—finding ways to uncover great ideas—is exactly what any smart organization tries to do. Sam Walton was "systematizing serendipity" in the Saturday morning meetings. I have "systematized serendipity" with my curiosity conversations.

In the *Harvard Business Review* story on P&G, the word "innovation" appears sixty-five times. The word curiosity: not once.[11]

That's crazy. We simply don't credit curiosity. We don't even credit curiosity when we're using it, describing it, and extolling it.

The way we talk about this is revealing and important. You can't understand, appreciate, and cultivate something if you don't even acknowledge that it exists. How can we teach kids to be curious if we don't use the word curiosity? How can we encourage curiosity at work if we don't tell people to be curious?

It's not a trivial, semantic argument.

We live in a society that is increasingly obsessed with "innovation" and "creativity."

Twenty years ago, in 1995, "innovation" was mentioned about eighty times a day in the U.S. media; "creativity" was mentioned ninety times a day.

Just five years later, the mentions of "innovation" had soared to 260 a day; "creativity" was showing up 170 times a day.

By 2010, "innovation" was showing up 660 times a day, creativity close behind at 550 mentions a day.

Curiosity gets only a quarter of those mentions in the daily media—in 2010, about 160 times a day. That is, curiosity gets as many mentions today as "creativity" and "innovation" did a decade ago.[12]

The big U.S. universities maintain online databases of their faculty "experts," so media and business can consult them. MIT lists nine faculty members who consider themselves experts on creativity, and twenty-seven who are experts on innovation. MIT experts on curiosity? Zero. Stanford lists four faculty experts on creativity, and twenty-one on innovation. Stanford faculty offering to talk about curiosity? Zero.

It's essential to cultivate creativity and innovation, of course. That's what has driven our economy forward, that's what so dramatically improves the way we live—in everything from telephones to retailing, from medicine to entertainment, from travel to education.

But as indispensable as they are, "creativity" and "innovation" are hard to measure and almost impossible to teach. (Have you ever met someone who once lacked the ability to be creative or innovative, took a course, and became creative and innovative?) In fact, we often don't agree on what constitutes an idea that is "creative" or "innovative." Nothing is as common as the innovation I come up with that I think is brilliant and you think is dumb.

I think that this intense focus on being creative and innovative can be counterproductive. The typical person at work in a cubicle may not think of himself or herself as being "creative" or "innovative." Those of us who don't work in the corporate research and development department may well be clear that "innovation" isn't our job—because right over in that other building is the "department of innovation." In fact, whether we might think we are creative or not, in most workplaces, it's pretty clear that creativity isn't part of our jobs—that's why customer service reps are reading to us from scripts when we call the 800 number, not actually talking to us.

Unlike creativity and innovation, though, curiosity is by its nature more accessible, more democratic, easier to see, and also easier to do.

From my own experience pitching hundreds of movie ideas to studio executives, I know just how often people get told "no" to their brilliant ideas—not just most of the time, but 90 percent of the time. It takes a strong stomach to absorb all that rejection, and I don't think most people feel like they get paid to come up with ideas that get rejected. (In the movie business, unfortunately, we don't get paid at all without having our ideas rejected, because the only way to get to "yes" is through a lot of "no's.")

Here's the secret that we don't seem to understand, the wonderful connection we're not making: Curiosity is the tool that sparks creativity. Curiosity is the technique that gets to innovation.

Questions create a mind-set of innovation and creativity. Curiosity presumes that there might be something new out there. Curiosity presumes that there might be something outside our own experience out there. Curiosity allows the possibility that the way we're doing it now isn't the only way, or even the best way.

I said in chapter 1 that curiosity is the flint that sparks great ideas for stories. But the truth is much broader: curiosity doesn't just spark stories, it sparks inspiration in whatever work you do.

You can always be curious. And curiosity can pull you along until you find a great idea.

Sam Walton didn't walk the aisles of his own store trying to be inspired to do something new. That would have been as useful as looking inside empty Wal-Mart tractor trailers for inspiration. He needed a different perspective on the world—just like I found with Chief Gates or Lew Wasserman. Sam Walton wanted to innovate in the most ordinary of settings—a store. He started by being curious about everyone else in retailing. He just kept asking that question over and over again: what are our competitors doing?

I don't sit in my office, gazing out the windows at Beverly Hills, waiting for movie ideas to float into my field of vision. I talk to other people. I seek out their perspective and experience and stories, and by doing that I multiply my own experience a thousandfold.

What I do, in fact, is keep asking questions until something interesting happens.

That's something we can all do. We can teach people to ask good questions, we can teach people to listen to the answers, and we can teach people to use the answers to ask the next question. The first step, in fact, is to treat the questions themselves as valuable, as worth answering—starting with our own kids. If you treat the question with respect, the person asking it almost always listens to the answer with respect (even if they don't respect the actual answer).

Being curious and asking questions creates engagement. Using curiosity to disrupt your own point of view is almost always worthwhile, even when it doesn't work out the way you expect.

That's part of the fun of curiosity—you are supposed to be surprised. If you only get the answers you anticipate, you're not being very curious. When you get answers that are surprising, that's how you know that you've disrupted your point of view. But being surprised can also be uncomfortable, and I know that well.

As I said, one of the people I was determined to meet and have a curiosity conversation with when I was just starting out in the movie business was Edward Teller. Teller was a towering figure from my youth, although not necessarily in a good way.

He was a brilliant theoretical physicist who worked on the Manhattan Project, developing the first atomic bomb. One of the early worries about the bomb was that the nuclear reaction an atomic bomb started might never stop—that a single bomb might consume the entire Earth. It was Teller's calculations that proved an atomic bomb, while enormously destructive, would have a confined impact.

Teller went on to drive the creation of the hydrogen bomb—a thousand times more powerful than the atomic bomb. He became director of the nation's premier nuclear weapons research facility, Lawrence Livermore Laboratory in California. He was more than just brilliant, he was a vigorous advocate of a strong defense, and passionate about the importance of nuclear weapons to that defense.

By the time I was working as a movie producer, Teller was in his seventies, but he had found a fresh role advocating for and helping to design President Ronald Reagan's controversial Star Wars missile defense shield, formally called the Strategic Defense Initiative. Teller was a cantankerous, difficult personality—he was widely rumored to be the inspiration for the title character "Dr. Strangelove" in Stanley Kubrick's 1964 movie.

I wanted to meet him simply because I wanted to understand the personality of someone who could be passionate about inventing the most destructive weapon in the history of humanity.

It was, not surprisingly, almost impossible to get an appointment with Teller. His office didn't respond to telephone calls at all. I wrote letters. I wrote follow-up letters. I offered to fly to him. Finally, one day in 1987, I got a call. Dr. Teller—who was then seventy-nine and working on Star Wars—would be passing through Los Angeles. He would have a layover of a few hours, and would be spending those hours in a hotel near LAX. I could see him for an hour if I wanted to come to the hotel.

Two military officers were waiting for me in the hotel lobby, in dress uniforms. They rode up with me. Teller had a suite of two adjoining rooms, and there were other military staff and aides. I didn't see him alone.

Right from the start, he seemed pretty scary to me.

He was short. And he was indifferent. He didn't seem interested in my being there at all. You know, if people are interested in you, or if they simply want to be polite, they radiate some energy. Daryl Gates certainly had some energy.

Not Teller.

That indifference, of course, makes it hard to talk to someone.

He did seem to know that I had been trying to make an appointment with him for a year. It irritated him. He started out crabby, and we didn't move much beyond that.

He was clearly very smart and professorial, but in a high-handed kind of way. I tried to ask him about his weapons work, but I didn't get very far. What he said was, "I advance technologies as far as they can be advanced. And that's my mission."

In our conversation, he exuded a barrier similar to the one he was talking about creating over the North American continent. There was an invisible glass wall between us.

He was sending a very clear message: I was not important to him. I was wasting his time.

To be honest, what you're hoping for when you meet someone like Teller—who has had this incredible impact on the events that have shaped the world—what you're hoping for, really, is some kind of secret.

The secret to global security, or American security.

The secret to who they are.

You're hoping for some kind of insight—a gesture, an attitude.

That expectation is a little grandiose, of course. It's hard to get secrets from someone with whom you spend forty-five minutes.

But it felt like I got nothing but scorn from Teller.

I asked him about television. He said, "I don't do that."

I asked him about the movies. He said, "I don't see movies. The last movie I saw was fifty years ago. It was *Dumbo.*"

The great nuclear physicist had seen one of my precious moving pictures once, half a century earlier. *Dumbo.* A cartoon about a flying elephant.

He was actually saying that he didn't think what I did had any value. He certainly didn't care about storytelling. It wasn't just that he didn't care about it—he had contempt for it. In that sense, I was kind of offended by him. Why bother to see me, just to be rude to me? But I was really only offended in a part of my mind. I was mostly fascinated by his contempt.

In the end, he certainly qualified as disruptive—he really reached me in a way I'll never forget.

Teller was clearly a passionate patriot—almost a zealot. He cared about the United States, he cared about freedom, and in his own way, he cared about humanity.

But what was so interesting, when I had time to think about it, was that he himself seemed to lack humanity, to be immune to ordinary human connection.

When I met Teller, I was already well established as a movie producer. But you leave a meeting like that humbled, to be sure. I felt kind of like I'd been kicked in the stomach.

That doesn't mean I regretted chasing Edward Teller for a year. In a way I hadn't expected, his personality kind of matched his achievements. But that's the point of curiosity—you don't always get what you think you're going to get.

And just as important, you don't necessarily know how your curiosity is going to be received. Not everyone appreciates being the target of curiosity, and that too is a way of seeing the world from someone else's point of view.

In truth, though, I got exactly what I was hoping for: I got a vivid sense of Edward Teller. I got exactly the message Dr. Teller was sending about our relative places in the world.

Curiosity is risky. But that's good. That's how you know how valuable it is.

CHAPTER THREE

The Curiosity Inside the Story

"Human minds yield helplessly to the suction of story."

—*Jonathan Gottschall*[1]

WHEN VERONICA DE NEGRI NARRATES the story of her life, it's hard to connect the details of what you're hearing with the quiet, composed woman who is standing alongside you.

De Negri was a bookkeeper for a paper company, living with her husband and two young sons in Valparaíso, Chile, a historic five-hundred-year-old port city that is so beautiful its nickname is "the Jewel of the Pacific."

In her spare time, de Negri worked with trade unions and women's groups in Valparaíso, and in the early 1970s, she also worked for the government of Chile's democratically elected president, Salvador Allende.

Allende was overthrown in 1973 by the man he had appointed to lead Chile's military, General Augusto Pinochet. The coup was so violent that at one point, Chilean air force planes flew bombing runs against their nation's own Presidential Palace in Santiago in an effort to dislodge Allende. Pinochet assumed power on September 11, 1973, and immediately started rounding up and "disappearing" Chileans he saw as opponents, or even potential opponents.

Perhaps because of her trade-union work, or her work for Allende, officers from Chilean marine intelligence finally came for de Negri in 1975, taking her from her apartment to a marine intelligence base in Valparaíso. She was twenty-nine years old, her sons were eight and two. Her husband was also taken that day.

At the time, Pinochet's forces were arresting, imprisoning, and torturing so many Chileans—40,000 in all—that the dictator had to set up a network of concentration camps across Chile to handle them.

De Negri was first held at the marine base in Valparaíso. After several months, she was moved to a concentration camp in Santiago. At both places, she was tortured systematically, relentlessly, almost scientifically—day after day for months.

I met Veronica de Negri in the most unlikely of settings:

the beach in Malibu, California. In the late 1980s, I lived in Malibu Beach, and my neighbors included the musician Sting and his wife, Trudie Styler. One Sunday afternoon, they invited a small group to their beachfront house for dinner.

"I want you to meet somebody," Sting said to me. "Veronica de Negri. She was incarcerated and tortured in Chile by Pinochet." Sting was working with Amnesty International, and had gotten to know Veronica well through the organization.

Veronica at that point had moved to Washington, DC. After being released from the concentration camp in Santiago, then rearrested several times to remind her that she was being watched, she was expelled from Chile, and reunited with her sons in Washington, who were in high school and junior high. When we met that day at Sting's home, Veronica's torturer, Pinochet, was still in power in Chile.

We started talking, and then we went for a walk on the beach.

For much of the time she was imprisoned, Veronica was blindfolded. Her torturers were devastatingly clever. Most of what was inflicted on Veronica was done episodically and erratically. So even when she wasn't being actively tortured, she lived in a state of sickening fear, because she knew that at any moment, the door of her cell could fly open, and she could be hauled off for another round. It didn't matter what time it was. It didn't matter whether the last torture session had ended an hour earlier, or three days earlier. The next round could always be just a tick of the clock away.

Pinochet's men had contrived to make sure that Veronica was being tortured psychologically, even if they didn't have the staff at that moment to torture her physically.

They used the same technique to make the torture itself more unbearable. One thing Veronica was subjected to was something she called "submarines." A tank was filled with the ugliest water imaginable, mixed with urine, feces, and other garbage. Veronica was bound, and the rope holding her was threaded through a pulley at the bottom of the tank. She was held just above the surface of the tank and then yanked down to the bottom, where she had to hold her breath until she was allowed to surface amid the stench of what was in the water. The time held underwater was never the same, the time at the surface to catch her breath was never the same.

She said that the unpredictability was almost worse than whatever was done to her: How long am I going to be able to breathe? How long am I going to have to hold my breath, and can I hold my breath that long?

It's one thing to hear about human cruelty on the news, or to read about it. But to walk alongside Veronica de Negri and hear what other human beings had done to her is an experience unlike any I had ever had before.

How does a person do that to another person?

Where does the strength come from to survive?

It takes enormous courage just to be able to retell that story to a stranger—to relive what was done, and also to absorb the reaction of the person hearing the story.

I was completely mesmerized by Veronica because of that courage, and also because of her self-possession and her dignity. Her refusal to be silent. She opened to me a world I would never have been aware of, and a whole set of human qualities and behaviors I would never have thought about.

Veronica de Negri gave me something critical in addition to the searing details of her story. She gave me a completely new sense of human resilience.

One of the concepts that really animates me is what I think of as "mastery." I want to know what it takes to really master something—not just to be a police officer, but to be the chief; not just to be an intelligence agent, but to be head of the CIA; not just to be a trial attorney, but to be F. Lee Bailey. That's a quiet thread through my curiosity, and it's also a theme in some form of every one of my movies. The stories touch the whole range of human experience, I hope, but the central struggle is often about achievement, or the struggle for achievement. What does success look like, what does success *feel* like, to a father or the president of the United States, a rap musician or a mathematician?

Veronica de Negri really shattered the question of "mastery" for me. Of anyone I have ever met, she faced the most fearsome and enormous personal challenge. But it was also the most basic. She wasn't trying to solve a math equation. She was trying to survive. She was trying to survive in the face of smart, evil people who wanted to destroy her.

For Veronica, there was no help. There was no rescue. She

was up against the most horrifying opponent—well-armed fellow human beings. The stakes were total: her sanity and her physical survival. And the only person she could turn to was herself. She had to search inside herself for the skills she needed to withstand what was done to her. Nothing else was available—not even a view of what she was facing beyond the blindfold.

I met and talked to Veronica several times after that first meeting at Sting's house. Over time, what I came to understand was that she had found a capacity inside herself that most of us never go looking for, let alone have to depend on.

The only way to persevere is to have the capacity to calmly separate yourself from what is being done to you.

Veronica figured out that to withstand being tortured, she had to take herself out of the reality of what was being done to her. You slow your brain down, you slow yourself down. People talk about being in "flow," when they're writing, when they're surfing or rock-climbing or running, when they're lost in doing something completely absorbing.

What Veronica told me is that to survive being tortured, hour after hour, every day for eight months, she had to get into a state of flow as well, but a flow state of an alternate reality, that has its own narrative. That's how she survived. She couldn't control the physical world, but she could control her psychological reaction to it.

It's a mechanism, and it's how she saved herself. In fact, it's a storytelling mechanism. You have to find a different story to tell yourself to take you out of the torture.

Veronica's story is so compelling that we tried to capture it in a movie, *Closet Land*. *Closet Land* has just two characters—a woman and her torturer. It was always going to have a small audience, because it is so intense, so unrelenting. But I wanted to do a movie that gets viewers inside the mind of someone who is being tortured. Torture takes place all over the planet, and I wanted people to be able to see it.

What I learned from Veronica, her sense of mastery, connects to the psychology of the characters in many other movies and shows. When I first read astronaut Jim Lovell's account of the explosion and crisis on the Apollo 13 capsule, I couldn't really grasp the details of the spacecraft, the orbital mechanics, the issues with fuel and carbon dioxide and skipping off the top of Earth's atmosphere. What I connected with immediately was the sense Lovell conveyed of being trapped, of being in a physical setting, also a life-or-death setting, where he and his fellow astronauts had lost control. They had to adopt a mind-set like Veronica's—they had to create an alternate narrative—to have the psychological strength to get themselves back to Earth. I think that movie, too, owes a lot to Veronica de Negri.

You might expect someone who had survived what Veronica was put through to be discouraged, to be cynical, to lack a certain basic hope.

She isn't like that at all. She's vibrant. She's a person of intellect, and obviously a person of inner strength. She isn't cheery or buoyant, but she has great energy, fierce energy.

And she has this incredible human capacity to rely on her

own psychic strength to survive. That's what is so urgent to me about people's emotional makeup. What saved Veronica was her character, her personality, the story she was able to tell herself.

. . .

CURIOSITY CONNECTS YOU TO reality.

I live in two overlapping worlds that are often far from reality: the world of Hollywood show business, and the world of storytelling. In Hollywood, we have a sense of being at the center of the world. Our creative work touches everyone in the United States, as well as a huge part of the rest of the world. We deal with actors and directors who are famous and, in Hollywood, powerful—powerful in that they can demand large paychecks, they can command armies of staff and technicians, they can pick their work, they can create whole new worlds from scratch, and they can specify all kinds of quirky elements about things like the food they'll eat. Our projects involve huge sums of money—both the dollars to get a project made in the first place, and the dollars they make when they succeed in theaters and on TV. The millions are often in the triple digits, and we're now firmly in the era of the billion-dollar film franchise, and the era of the billion-dollar acting career.[2]

So Hollywood absolutely has a huge sense of importance about what we do, and we have a huge sense of importance about the people who do it. It's possible to lose track of the difference between the stories we're telling, with as much vividness and texture as we can possibly create, and the real world. For while the money is real—the risks are real, and they are often large—the rest of it is, of course, showbiz, make-believe.

A comedy about the New York City morgue—*Night Shift*—doesn't involve any dead bodies.

A TV drama about producing a sports news show—*Sports Night*—involves no sporting events, no sports figures, no news.

A movie about the brutal reality of drug smuggling—*American Gangster*—involves no actual drugs or brutality.

Even in a great love story, no one typically falls in love.

Just as important, storytelling itself is not reality. That may seem obvious, but it's not at all. When you come home from work and tell your wife or husband "the story" of your day, you reshape those nine hours to highlight the drama, to make your own role the centerpiece, to leave out the boring parts (which may be eight hours of the nine). And you're telling a real story about your real day.

In the movies and on TV, we're always trying to tell stories that are true—whether it's *Frost/Nixon*, about real people and real events, or *How the Grinch Stole Christmas!*, about a child's fantasy. The stories need to be "true" in emotional terms, true in thematic terms, not necessarily true in factual terms. For any movie that purports to tackle a set of real events, there's now typically a website detailing all the things we "got wrong"—

you can read about the departures from reality in *Gravity* and *Captain Phillips*. We released *Apollo 13* in the summer of 1995—before Google was on the Internet—but you can read about the ways the movie differs from the factual story of the rescue at a half dozen websites.[3] You can even read about the differences between 2014's movie *Noah* with Russell Crowe, and the biblical Noah, that is, the differences between the movie and the "real" story of a mythic biblical figure.[4]

The truth is, we want to tell great stories, captivating stories, and so we tweak the stories all the time—in fact, when we're making a movie or a TV show, we tweak the stories every day, while we're making them—in order to get more immediacy, or to move things along more quickly. We tweak them to make them seem more realistic, even when we're actually deviating from the "facts." We're all storytellers, and in about the third grade we start to learn the difference between a story that is true and a story that is factually correct.

It is very easy to get caught up in the urgency and the charisma of Hollywood. It's a hermetic world (it doesn't help that we're in California, far from a lot of the big decision making in Washington, DC, and New York City). It's very easy to get caught up in the world of episodic storytelling.

Curiosity pulls me back to reality. Asking questions of real people, with lives outside the movie business, is a bracing reminder of all the worlds that exist beyond Hollywood.

You can make as many movies as you want about war or black ops or revolution or prison. They're just movies. What was done to Veronica de Negri was not a movie, it was real—her pain and her survival.

. . .

WHEN YOU WATCH A movie that is completely engrossing, what happens to you? I'm talking about one of those movies where you lose track of time, where everything fades away except the fate of the characters, and their world, on screen. One of those movies where you walk out onto the sidewalk afterward, blinking, reentering reality, thinking, Wow, it's a Sunday afternoon in spring. Whew.

When you binge-watch the latest episodes of *Arrested Development* or *House of Cards*, what causes you to touch the PLAY button just one more time, six times in a row?

When you read a book, what keeps you in the chair, turning pages way past the moment when you should have set the book down and gone to sleep?

National Public Radio knows exactly how riveting its radio storytelling can be. NPR has figured out that people often park, turn off the engine, then sit in the car in the driveway, waiting to hear the end of a particular story that isn't quite finished. NPR calls these "driveway moments."[5] Why would anyone put the last three minutes of a story on NPR ahead of going inside to dinner and their family?

Curiosity.

Curiosity keeps you turning the pages of the book, it tugs

you along to watch just one more episode, it causes you to lose track of the day and the time and the weather when you're in a theater seat. Curiosity creates NPR's "driveway moments."[6]

Curiosity is a vital piece of great storytelling—the power of a story to grab hold of your attention, to create the irresistible pull of that simple question: what's going to happen next?

Good stories have all kinds of powerful elements. They have fascinating characters caught in revealing or meaningful or dramatic dilemmas. They have talented acting, good writing, and vivid voices. They have plots that are surprising, with great pacing and settings that transport you to the story's location. They create a world into which you can slip effortlessly—and then lose yourself.

But it's all in service of one goal: Making you care. You can say you care about the characters or the story, but all you really care about is what's going to happen next. What's going to happen in the end? How is the tangle of plot lines going to be untangled? How is the tangle of human relationships going to be untangled?

A story may or may not make its point memorably. It may or may not be entertaining or compelling, funny or sad, upsetting, even enraging.

But none of those qualities matter if you don't get the whole story—if you don't actually watch the movie or read the book. If you don't stick around, it doesn't matter what the point of the story is. To be effective, a story has to keep you in the chair—whether you're holding a Kindle, or sitting in your car with your hand on the radio knob, or sitting in the multiplex.

Inspiring curiosity is the first job of a good story.

How often have you started reading a newspaper or magazine story with a great headline, about a topic you care about, only to give up after a few paragraphs, thinking, *That story didn't live up to the headline.*

Curiosity is the engine that provides the momentum of good storytelling. But I think there's an even more powerful connection between them.

Storytelling and curiosity are really indispensable to each other. They certainly reinforce and refresh each other. But they might actually do more. Curiosity helps create storytelling. And there's no question storytelling inspires curiosity.

Curiosity is fun and enriching personally, in isolation. But the value and the fun of curiosity are magnified by sharing what you've learned. If you go to the zoo and see the new panda cubs, or you go to Florence and spend three days looking at Renaissance art, there's nothing like coming home and telling your family and friends "the story" of your trip. We read aloud the most amazing tidbits from the newspaper over breakfast. Half of what's on Twitter is literally people saying, "Look what I just read—can you believe this?" Someone's Twitter stream is a tour through what that person thinks is interesting enough to share—a journey through their version of clickable curiosity.

If you go all the way back in time to the earliest human

tribes, some kind of storytelling was indispensable to survival. The person who discovered the nearby spring of water had to communicate that. The mother who had to snatch her wandering child from the stalking cougar had to communicate that. The person who first found wild potatoes and figured out how to eat them had to communicate that.

Curiosity is great, but if what we learn evaporates, if it goes no further than our own experience, then it doesn't really help us.

Curiosity itself is essential to survival.

But the power of human development comes from being able to share what we learn, and to accumulate it.

And that's what stories are: shared knowledge.

Curiosity motivates us to explore and discover. Storytelling allows us to share the knowledge and excitement of what we've figured out. And that storytelling in turn inspires curiosity in the people to whom we're talking.

If you learn about the nearby spring, you may immediately be curious about trying to find it yourself. If you hear about this new food, the potato, you may be curious if you can cook it, and what it will taste like.

Even modern stories that are emotionally satisfying often leave you curious. How many people watch Ron Howard's *Apollo 13*—which has a deeply satisfying ending—then want to learn more about that mission, or the Apollo program and spaceflight in general?

There is, of course, a profession that connects curiosity and storytelling: journalism. That's what being a reporter is. But, in fact, we're all storytellers. We're all journalists and novelists of our own lives and relationships. Twitter, Instagram, and blogging are modern ways of saying "Here's what's happening in my life." What is the old-fashioned family dinner table but a kind of nightly news roundup of your family?

Much of the power of stories comes from their emotional heft. That's where the humor and the joy are, the excitement and the unforgettableness. We learn how to behave, in part, from the stories of how other people behave—whether those stories are told by sixth-grade girls over lunch, or by software engineers whose product didn't succeed with a new customer, or by Jane Austen in her novel *Sense and Sensibility*. Stories are how we learn about the world, but also how we learn about other people, about what's going on in their heads, and how it differs from what's going on in our heads.

From the moment we're born, from the moment we wake up in the morning, we're saturated in stories. Even when we're asleep, our brains are telling us stories.

One of the great unresolved questions of life on Earth is: why are humans able to make such great intellectual and social progress, compared to other animals?

Maybe it's the opposable thumb.

Maybe it's the size and structure of our brains.

Maybe it's language.

Maybe it's our ability to seize and use fire.

But maybe what makes humans unique is our ability to tell

stories—and our reflex to constantly connect curiosity and storytelling in an M. C. Escher–like spiral. Our stories and our curiosity mirror each other. They are what make us successful, and also human.

· · ·

WHEN I WAS GROWING up, my reading ability was severely impaired.

I couldn't read at all in my early years of elementary school. I'd look at the words on the page, but they made no sense. I couldn't sound them out, I couldn't connect the symbols printed there with the language I knew and used every day.

Back in the 1950s, when I was young, there were only two reasons you couldn't read in the third grade. You were stupid, or you were stubborn. But I was just baffled, and frustrated, and always worried about school.

People didn't start talking about dyslexia until ten years after I was in third grade and they didn't start really helping typical kids with it until ten years after that. Today, I might have been classified as dyslexic.

As it was, I got Fs in elementary school, with the occasional D. My savior was my grandmother—my mom's mother Sonia, a classic 4-foot-10 Jewish grandmother. She was always telling me I was something special.

My mother was upset—her son was failing third grade! She went off and found me a reading tutor, who slowly taught me to lasso the letters and the words on the page. My grandmother, on the other hand, was totally imperturbable. It was a real counterpoint.

She just kept telling me, "You're curious. Your curiosity is good. Think big!" My grandmother could see beyond the report card; it felt like she could see inside my head. She knew I was as hungry to learn as every other kid. I just had a hard time satisfying that hunger.

My grandmother really helped make me something of a dreamer. She said to me, "Don't let the system define you. You're already defined—you're curious!"

What a thing to say to a boy in elementary school—"Don't let the system define you!" But thank goodness she did. My grandmother taught me a lot, but one of the most important things she imparted was that all you really need is one champion.

When you can't read, and then when you've learned to read with real effort, a couple of things happen. First, in school, you hide out. If you can't do the reading, you can't answer the teacher's questions in class. So I was always ducking, not raising my hand, trying to be invisible. I was trying to avoid being humiliated.

When reading is hard work, you're cut off from the ease with which people learn by reading. And you're cut off from stories. For most people, reading is simply an unthinking tool—sometimes it's hard, when the material is hard, but often it's a source of joy or fun or pleasure. It's always a source of great stories.

But reading itself was so hard for me, I didn't curl up with a book just for fun, just to be carried off to a different world the way so many kids are—and adults, too, of course. And I couldn't decide the way a sixth grader might that I was interested in something—the solar system, whales, Abe Lincoln—and go check out a stack of books on that topic from the library.

I had to be resourceful to learn what I wanted to learn, and also patient and determined.

My reading ability gradually improved throughout high school. If what I had was dyslexia, I seemed to grow out of it as I grew up. As an adult, I do read—I read scripts and newspapers, books and magazines, memos and email. But every page is an effort. The work never fades. Reading for me, reading for someone who is dyslexic, I think, is a little bit like what math is for many people: you have to work so hard at getting the problem into your brain that you can lose track of the point of the problem itself. Even today, in my sixties, the physical effort of reading drains some of the pleasure I might take from whatever it is I'm reading.

What I think is amazing is that, despite my struggle with reading, two vital things survived: the joy I find in learning, and my passion for stories. I was the kid who wanted nothing more than to avoid questions in the classroom, and now I relish the chance to be an eager student, to ask questions of people who are themselves discovering the answers.

I was the kid who didn't have the pleasure of losing himself in all those great growing-up classics—*James and the Giant*

Peach, Charlotte's Web, Dune, A Wrinkle in Time, The Catcher in the Rye—but now I spend my life helping create exactly those kinds of completely absorbing stories, just on screen.

I love good stories, I just like them best the way they were originally discovered—told out loud. That's why the curiosity conversations have been so important to me, and also so much fun. I've described some of the dramatic ones, but most of the conversations have taken place in my office. Some of them have been like reading a story from the front page of the *Wall Street Journal*, perfectly crystallizing something in a way I'll never forget.

I've always been interested in manners and etiquette: What's the right way to behave, what's the right way to treat people? Why does it matter who opens the door and where the silverware sits on the table?

I invited Letitia Baldrige in to talk—the legendary expert on protocol of every kind who first became famous as social secretary for Jacqueline Kennedy, helping turn the Kennedy White House into a center of culture and the arts. Baldrige had left Tiffany & Co. to go to work at the White House, and she went on to write a newspaper column and many books on modern manners. She was tall—much taller than I am—and already silver-haired when she came to talk. She entered my office with elegant authority.

Letitia Baldrige gave me an understanding of the difference between "manners" and "etiquette"—something I had never quite grasped before.

Manners are really the basis for how we treat other people—manners are born out of compassion, empathy, the "golden rule." Manners are, quite simply, making people feel welcome, comfortable, and respected.

Etiquette is the set of techniques you use to have great manners. Etiquette is the by-product. The way you invite someone to an event makes a difference. The way you greet people, the way you introduce them to people already present, the way you pull a chair out for someone.

Manners are the way you want to behave, and the way you want to make people feel. Etiquette is the granularization of that desire to treat people with grace and warmth.

I love that distinction. For me, it illuminates both manners and etiquette, making them more understandable and more practical. I use a little bit of what Letitia Baldrige taught me every day. You open the car door for your partner not because she can't open the door herself, but because you love her. You arrange the silverware on the table a certain way because that gives your guests comfort and predictability so they can be more relaxed at dinner.

And as Letitia told me, the feeling you're trying to convey—the hospitality, the warmth—is much more important than following any particular rule. You can follow the rules, but if you do it with a disdainful attitude, you're being rude, despite having "perfect" etiquette.

Not every conversation was so practically useful. One of my favorites was with someone who, at first glance, would seem to be the exact opposite of etiquette expert Letitia Baldrige:

Sheldon Glashow, the Harvard physicist who won the Nobel Prize in physics in 1979 when he was forty-six years old, for research he did when he was twenty-eight.

We flew Glashow out to Los Angeles from Cambridge. He came to the office one morning, and he seemed as delighted at the novelty of meeting someone with influence in the movie business as I was to meet someone of his stature from the world of science.

When he came to visit, in 2004, he was seventy-two, one of the wise men of modern particle physics. Glashow's pioneering work in physics involved figuring out that what physicists thought were the four basic forces of nature might actually be three forces—he helped "unify" the weak force and the electromagnetic force. (The other two are the strong force and gravity.)

I enjoy trying to wrap my brain around particle physics. I like it the same way some people like to understand the complexities of geology or currency trading or poker. It's an arcane world all its own, with a distinct language and cast of characters—particle physics can literally seem like a different universe. And yet, it's the universe we live in. We're all made up of quarks and hadrons and electroweak forces.

Walking into my office, Glashow couldn't have been more enthusiastic or open. I'm a layman, but he was happy to talk me through the science of where particle physics is today. He has the demeanor of your favorite, patient professor. If you don't quite understand something, he'll try explaining it in a different way.

He's a teacher as well as a scientist. The morning Glashow

won the Nobel Prize, he had to cancel his 10 a.m. class—which was on particle physics—for Harvard undergraduates.

Glashow was curious about the movie business. He clearly likes movies. He'd helped Matt Damon and Ben Affleck get the math right for *Good Will Hunting* (he's thanked in the credits).

Glashow was the opposite of Edward Teller. He welcomed the chance to talk—he did give up two days to make time to visit—and he was interested in just about everything. We typically put the conversations on the day's schedule for an hour or two. Shelly Glashow and I talked for four hours, and it just flew by. The main feeling I had when I walked Dr. Glashow out of the office was, I'd like to talk to this man again.

A newspaper or magazine story, in the hands of a talented reporter, could have captured much of what I got from Letitia Baldrige and Sheldon Glashow. But I would have been working so hard at the reading, I think I would have missed the fun.

I understand every time that my curiosity conversations are a remarkable privilege—most people don't have a life that allows them to call people and invite them in to talk. But I get something special out of this kind of curiosity that isn't unique to me, or to this particular setting: meeting people in person is totally different from seeing them on TV, or reading about them. That's not just true for me. The vividness of someone's personality and energy really only comes alive when you shake hands and look them in the eye. When you hear them tell a story. That has a real emotional power for me, and a real staying power. It's learning without being taught, it's learning through storytelling.

That kind of direct, in-person curiosity allows you to be surprised. Both Baldrige and Glashow were surprising—much different than I might have imagined in advance.

Baldrige was focused on manners, not etiquette. For all her experience at the highest levels of what you might call precision protocol—from Tiffany to state dinners at the White House—she really just wanted people to treat each other well. She was the legendary arbiter of the rules, but for her, manners weren't about the rules, they were about grace and hospitality.

Glashow works in an area of science that is so arcane, it requires as many years of school *after* high school graduation as before, just to get to the point where you can start making fresh progress. And yet he was the opposite of inaccessible and insular. It was refreshing to meet a brilliant theoretical physicist who wasn't at all the cliché of the distracted scientist. He was completely engaged in the wider world.

My point is that you don't actually need to be sitting down, by appointment, with the social secretary of the White House or the Nobel Prize–winning physicist to have that kind of experience. When someone new joins your company, when you're standing on the sidelines at your son's soccer game alongside the other parents, when you're on an airplane seated next to a stranger, or attending a big industry conference, all these people around you have tales to tell. It's worth giving yourself the chance to be surprised.

•   •   •

I MET CONDOLEEZZA RICE at a dinner party in Hollywood. I'd always been intrigued by her. She's a classical pianist. She was a professor of political science at Stanford University, and then the university's provost—the chief academic officer. And of course she was President George W. Bush's national security advisor for four years and secretary of state for four years. She has remarkable presence—given her level of responsibility, she always appears composed, even calm. She also conveys a sense of being in the know. To me, she almost seemed to have superpowers.

The dinner where I met her was in 2009, not long after she had stepped down as secretary of state. She was sitting just across from me.

Condi still had security shadowing her, but she was very easy to talk to. One thing you see up close that you never saw when she was speaking on TV is the sparkle in her eyes. As the dinner was breaking up, I said to her, "Can I call you? Maybe you'll have lunch with me?"

She smiled and said, "Sure."

Not long after, we had lunch at E Baldi, on Cañon Drive, a well-known Hollywood restaurant. She arrived in a car with her security detail, and we sat in the only booth in the small restaurant.

Condi was relaxed and gracious, but I think I was more curious about her than she was about me.

I told her about a movie we were getting ready to make. It was called *Cartel*, about a man bent on revenge against the Mexican drug cartels after they brutally murder his wife. The movie was set in Mexico, the seat of so much cartel violence, and we were going to film it in Mexico, just a couple of months away. We originally had Sean Penn set to star; when he couldn't do it, we got Josh Brolin for the lead. I was worried about filming a movie sharply critical of the cartels, in the country where they were beheading judges.

Condi listened. I told her that studio security had assessed the areas where we wanted to film in Mexico and told us it was fine. She looked at me skeptically. "I don't think it's safe to do that," she said.

Cartel was at a crossroads. We had spent money. The studio thought it was safe. But what I read in the newspapers every day suggested something different. The issue of safety nagged at me. I thought, Would I personally travel to the set of a cartel movie in Mexico? Answering honestly, I thought I wouldn't. And if I wouldn't go, how could I be comfortable sending any-one else? I really needed another informed point of view.

Condi followed up after our lunch. She had done some checking and she said, "No. It's not safe to do what you're plan-ning."

That was the final straw, for me and the studio. We shut the movie down. We never took it to Mexico, it never got made. Looking back, I worry someone might have gotten killed. I've learned to pay attention to those instincts, to those occasional nagging doubts, and I've learned to make sure we're curious enough to find really expert opinion when there's a big risk. I think making a movie about drug cartels, in the nation where they were operating, could have been a disaster.

I wouldn't be very good at my job without curiosity. It's infused into every step of the process now. But think about the number of people who should also say that, in professions we don't typically think of as requiring inquisitiveness—at least as the primary skill—the way we expect it in a doctor or a detective.

A good financial planner needs to know the markets and the way to arrange money for retirement, but he also should be curious.

A good real estate agent needs to know the market, the houses available, the houses that might become available, but should also be curious about her clients.

A city planner needs to be curious, and an advertising executive, a housekeeper, a fitness trainer, a car mechanic, a good hairstylist all need to be curious as well.

And in every case, the curiosity is all about the story. What's the story of your life, and how are you hoping that money or a new house or a new hairstyle will help you shape that story, and help you tell it?

This kind of curiosity seems so routine that we shouldn't even need to talk about it. I think it used to be. But in a world where so many of our basic interactions are structured and scripted—we're talking to "customer service" on an 800 number, we're trying to be heard over the speaker in the drive-through lane, we're checking into a hotel where the hospitality is "trained"—curiosity has been strangled.

It's considered a wild card.

But that's exactly wrong. If you think about a good hairstylist, the job itself requires skill at understanding hair, at understanding the shapes of people's heads, the quality of their hair; and it has a spritz of creativity and individualism. But it's also got an important human element. As a customer, you want a stylist who is interested in you, who asks what your hair means to you, and who pays attention to how you want to look and feel when you stand up from the chair. You also want a stylist who talks to you, who asks the kinds of questions that keep both of you engaged and entertained while your hair is being washed and cut and dried. (Or a stylist who is perceptive enough to realize you don't want to talk at all.)

The great thing is that this perfectly routine sort of curiosity works for both the stylist and the customer. The customer gets the haircut she's hoping for, she gets hair that helps her present her best self, that helps her tell her story, and she also gets a fun, relaxing experience. The stylist avoids falling into a rut. She learns something about her customer, and also about how the world works—every customer in the styling chair is a chance for a miniature curiosity conversation. She's giving the best haircuts she can give while creating happy and loyal customers and having an entertaining work life.

Going to the hair salon is not like sitting down with an architect to plan the redesign of office space at your company, or to plan the addition to your house. But curiosity and storytelling add just a little bit of fun and distinctiveness—and occasionally learning and insight—to what can otherwise become routine.

If manners are the lubricant that lets us all get along, curiosity is the shot of Tabasco that adds some spice, wakes us up, creates connection, and puts meaning into almost any encounter.

CHAPTER FOUR

Curiosity as a Superhero Power

"Curiosity will conquer fear even more than bravery will."

—*James Stephens*[1]

I WAS SITTING IN THE bar at the Ritz-Carlton in New York City, facing Central Park, with a man with the best muttonchop sideburns since President Martin Van Buren. I was having drinks with Isaac Asimov, the author who helped bring science and science fiction alive for a whole generation of Americans.

It was 1986, the movie *Splash* had come out and broken through, and I was using that success to make the curiosity conversations as ambitious as possible.

Isaac Asimov was a legend, of course. At the time we met, he had written more than 300 books. By the time he died, in 1992, that number had grown to 477. Asimov's writing is so clear and accessible—rendering all kinds of complicated topics understandable—that it's easy to overlook how smart he was. Although no one ever called him "Dr. Asimov," he had a PhD in chemistry from Columbia, and before he was able to support himself by writing, he was a professor of biochemistry at Boston University's medical school.

Most people know Asimov as a storyteller and a visionary, a man who was able to look at how science and human beings interacted and imagine the future, the author of *I, Robot* and *The Foundation Trilogy*. But Asimov actually wrote more non-fiction books than fiction. He wrote seven books about mathematics, he wrote sixty-eight books on astronomy, he wrote a biochemistry textbook, he wrote books titled *Photosynthesis* and *The Neutrino: Ghost Particle of the Atom*. He wrote literary guides to the Bible (two volumes), Shakespeare, and *Paradise Lost*. He had a boy's mischievous love of jokes and wrote eight books or collections of humor, including *Lecherous Limericks*, *More Lecherous Limericks*, and *Still More Lecherous Limericks*. In the last decade of his life, Asimov wrote fifteen or more books a year. He was writing books faster than most people can read them—including me.[2]

Asimov was a polymath, an autodidact, and a genius. And he was an instinctive storyteller. Who wouldn't want to sit down with him for an hour?

Isaac Asimov met me at the Ritz-Carlton with his second wife, Janet Jeppson Asimov, a psychiatrist with degrees from Stanford and NYU. I found her more intimidating than I found him—Isaac was relaxed, his wife was more on guard. She was clearly the boss, or at least his protector.

Both Isaac and Janet ordered ginger ale.

We started to chat. Apparently, it wasn't going that well, although I didn't quite realize how poorly it was going. After only ten minutes—the Asimovs hadn't even finished their ginger ales—Janet Asimov abruptly interrupted.

"You clearly don't know my husband's work well enough to have this conversation," she said, rising from the table. "This is a waste of his time. We're leaving. C'mon, Isaac."

And that was it. They got up and left me sitting alone at the table, mouth half-open in astonishment.

I had arranged a meeting with one of the most interesting, inventive, and prolific storytellers of our time, and I had managed to bore him (or, at least, bore his watchful wife) so thoroughly in just ten minutes that they couldn't bear it and had to flee the black hole of my dullness.[3]

I don't think I've ever felt so much like I had been slapped—without actually having been touched—in my life.

Here's the thing: Janet Asimov was right.

It took me a few months to get over the sting of them walking out. But she had caught me, and she had called me on it. I wasn't prepared well enough to talk to Isaac Asimov. He had agreed to take an hour to sit down with me—for him, that was a sacrifice of a whole book chapter—but I hadn't respected him in turn. I hadn't taken the time to learn enough about him, or to read, say, *I, Robot* from start to finish.

Going into that meeting, I was scared of Isaac Asimov. I was worried about exactly what ended up happening: I was afraid of not knowing enough to have a good conversation with Asimov. But I hadn't been smart enough to harness that fear to curiosity.

I never made those mistakes again.

I've learned to rely on curiosity in two really important ways: first, I use curiosity to fight fear.

I have a whole bunch of relatively ordinary fears.

I have a fear of public speaking.

I don't really love big social settings where I might not have a good time, where I might end up kind of trapped, or where I might not be as entertaining as someone thinks I should be.

Now, take a minute to consider this list. Given my fears, I sure have picked the wrong profession. Half my life—half my work life—requires me to go somewhere, give a talk, mingle in large social settings with important people who I kind of know, but not really.

Throw in that I'm a little scared of powerful people, and a little intimidated by intellectuals—exactly the kind of people with whom I want to have curiosity conversations—and it can seem like I've created a life that's perfectly designed to make me anxious from the moment I open my eyes in the morning.

In addition to using curiosity to tackle my fears, I use curiosity to instill confidence—in my ideas, in my decisions, in my vision, in myself. Hollywood, as I've mentioned, is the land of "no." Instead of spelling out the word H-O-L-L-Y-W-O-O-D in the famous sign in the Hollywood Hills, they could have spelled out: N-O-N-O-N-O-N-O!

An aspiring filmmaker was in my office recently for a meeting, and he said to me, "Oh, you're cool. No one ever says 'no' to you."

That's silly. Everybody says "no" to me. Everybody *still* says "no" to me. It's just the opposite of what it looks like.

Sure, people *like* me. People say "yes" to meetings.

People say, "Please come to dinner." Sometimes they say, "Please come on this cool trip with me"—and that's flattering.

But if I want to do something creative, if I want to do something edgy—a TV series about a medieval executioner, for instance, that I helped push forward in 2014, or a movie about the impact of James Brown on the music business in the United States, which came out in the summer of 2014, people say "no." These days, they just smile and put their arm around my shoulder when they do.

You have to learn to beat the "no."

Everybody in Hollywood has to beat the "no"—and if you write code in Silicon Valley, or if you design cars in Detroit, if you manage hedge funds in Lower Manhattan, you also have to learn to beat the "no."

Some people here charm their way around the "no."

Some people cajole their way around it, some people reason their way around it, some people whine their way around it.

If I need support on a project, I don't want to cajole or charm or wheedle anyone into it. I want them to have the same enthusiasm and commitment I feel. I don't want to pull someone in against his or her judgment. I want them to see the idea, the movie, the characters with the kind of excitement that carries them through the tough parts of any project.

I use curiosity to beat the "no," I use curiosity to figure out how to get to "yes." But not quite in the way you would imagine.

. . .

I DIDN'T TURN INTO a full-fledged producer with the first movie Ron Howard and I made—*Night Shift*. That movie was clever, sexy, and easy to explain. It had a quick hook. You could instantly see the comic possibilities. In fact, *Night Shift* is based on a real story I read in the back pages of the *New York Times* in the summer of 1976.[4]

It was the second movie Ron and I made together, *Splash*, that taught me what producers actually did in Hollywood. Their job is to come up with the vision of the story, and to find the financing and cast to make the movie, to protect the quality of the movie as it moves along. But first and foremost, the job of the producer is to get the movie made.

The kernel of *Splash*, what I call the "ignition point" for the story, is simple: what happens when a mermaid comes out of the ocean onto dry land?

What would her impressions be, what would her life be like? What would happen if I got to meet that mermaid? What would it take to win her love—what would she have to give up? What would a man wooing her have to give up?

I wrote the first script for *Splash* myself (I called it *Wet* to start with).

The mermaid idea came to me before the idea for *Night Shift*, while I was working as a producer of TV movies and miniseries (like *Zuma Beach* and the Ten Commandments series of TV movies). I was following the advice that Lew Wasserman gave me, to come up with ideas, something I could own, putting the pencil to the yellow legal pad. I was like any other twenty-eight-year-old man in the movie business in LA in the 1970s: I was enthralled with California women. I was always trying to understand them. It's not too far a leap from these bikini-clad women on the beach to a mermaid on the beach.

Except for this: no one wanted a movie about a mermaid.

No studio was interested, no director was interested.

Everybody said no.

Even Ron Howard didn't want to direct a movie about a mermaid. He said no more than once.

Hollywood is fundamentally a risk-averse town—we're always looking for the sure thing. That's why we have movies with four sequels, even six sequels.

No one seemed to understand a movie about a mermaid. Where was the previously successful mermaid movie, anyway?

Eventually two things happened.

First, I listened to the "no." There was information in the resistance that I had to be curious about.

I would say, "It's a movie about a mermaid, coming onto land. She meets a boy. It's funny!" That didn't work.

I would say, "It's a movie about a mermaid, coming onto land. She meets a boy. It's kind of a fantasy, you know?" They weren't buying it.

I needed to understand what people were saying no to. Were they saying no to a comedy? Were they saying no to a mermaid fantasy? Were they saying no to me—to Brian Grazer?

It turned out that I first wrote and pitched *Splash* too much from the perspective of the mermaid.

I thought mermaids were really intriguing, really alluring (and I'm in good company—see, for instance, Hans Christian Andersen's legendary *The Little Mermaid*). Hollywood studio executives just seemed puzzled. They were saying no to the mermaid.

So I thought, Okay, this isn't a mermaid movie—it's a love story! It's a romantic comedy with a mermaid as the girl. I *recontextualized* the movie. Same idea, different framework. I started pitching a movie that was a love story, between a man and a mermaid, with a little comedy thrown in.

The answer was still no, but a little less emphatic. You could see that at least executives were tickled by the idea of a love story involving a mermaid.

Anthea Sylbert, whose job was to buy movies for United Artists, was one of the people to whom I pitched *Splash*, more than once.

"I throw you out the door, you come back in the window," she told me with exasperation one day. "I throw you out the window, you come back down the chimney. The answer is no! I don't want this mermaid movie!"

I made a pest of myself. But as Anthea Sylbert recently told me, "You were a pest, but not like a mosquito. More like an overactive five-year-old. Impish. I kind of wanted to tell you to go sit in a corner and be quiet."

Despite saying no, Anthea was intrigued by the mermaid. "I've always been a sucker for mythology, for fables, for a fairy-tale kind of thing," she said. In fact, it wasn't too hard to make the mermaid movie into a mermaid-man love story, and from that into a mermaid-man-love-story-fairy-tale.

Anthea got me some money for a more polished script, and helped hire novelist and screenwriter Bruce Jay Friedman to rework my original version.

And I worked a little curiosity on Anthea too. She wanted rules for the mermaid.

I had no idea what she was talking about. "Why do we need rules?" I asked.

She wanted it clear how the mermaid behaved in the ocean,

and how she behaved on land (what happened to the tail, for instance?). She wanted the audience to be in on the rules.

"Why?" I asked again.

She thought it would add to both the fun and the fairy-tale element.

Then, out of nowhere, a second mermaid movie popped up—this one to be written by the legendary screenwriter Robert Towne (*Chinatown*, *Shampoo*), directed by Herbert Ross (*Goodbye, Mr. Chips*; *The Turning Point*), and it was going to star Warren Beatty and Jessica Lange.

One mermaid movie was totally uninteresting to Hollywood.

Two mermaid movies was one mermaid movie too many—and Hollywood was going with the one with the Oscar-winning writer and Oscar-nominated director. Especially over the partnership of Grazer and Howard—we had exactly one movie together to our credit.

I look laid-back, I dress laid-back, I try to act laid-back. But I'm not laid-back. I'm the guy who heard people talking about a job through an open window, and twenty-four hours later, I had that job. I can tick off several people whom I worked for six months to a year in order to arrange curiosity conversations: Lew Wasserman, Daryl Gates, Carl Sagan, Edward Teller, Jonas Salk.

So what happens first is that a dozen people tell me no one is interested in mermaids, no one is making a mermaid movie. Then people say, "Aww, I'm so sorry, we'd love to make your mermaid movie, but there's already a mermaid movie in the works—they've got Jessica Lange as the mermaid! Cool, huh? We wouldn't want to go head-to-head against *that*. Thanks for stopping by."

Sorry; I wasn't going to let Herbert Ross and Robert Towne do my mermaid movie.

Ron and I ended up striking a deal with Disney for *Splash* to be the first movie from their new division, Touchstone, which had been created specifically to give Disney the freedom to do grown-up movies. Ron not only signed up, he told Touchstone he would do the movie on a tight budget, and vowed to beat Herbert Ross's mermaid to theaters.

Splash was a huge hit. It was number one at the box office its first two weeks, it was in the top ten for eleven weeks, and it was at the time the fastest money-making movie in Disney film history. *Splash* was also the first Disney movie that wasn't rated G. We gave Disney a big PG-rated hit—the very first time.

We didn't just beat the other mermaid movie, it never got made. And *Splash* not only made money, it helped make the careers of Tom Hanks and Daryl Hannah. People in Hollywood went from being a little skeptical of Ron Howard as a director to elbowing each other out of the way to hire him.

And, in perhaps the sweetest moment, given how many times I heard the word "no" while trying to get it made, the script for *Splash* was nominated for an Academy Award for best original screenplay. That year, *Places in the Heart*, the movie about the Great Depression starring Sally Field, won. But Ron and I went to our first Academy Awards celebration.

The night *Splash* opened, March 9, 1984, Ron Howard and I hired a limousine and drove around with our wives, looking at the lines at LA movie theaters. That was a tradition we started with *Night Shift*, but those lines were a little disappointing. *Splash* was a different story.[5]

In Westwood, there was a theater called the Westwood Avco, right on Wilshire Boulevard. For the opening of Steven Spielberg's *E.T.*, in 1983, we had seen the lines at the Avco wrapped around the block. When we drove up the night *Splash* debuted, the lines were also around the block. Not as long as *E.T.*, but still incredible. People were standing in line to see our mermaid movie. It was thrilling. We jumped out of the car, and we walked from the front of the line to the back, talking to people and hugging each other.

Then we jumped back in the car and started another tradition: we drove to In-N-Out Burger, the famous Southern California drive-in, and ate burgers with a really good bottle of French Bordeaux I had been optimistic enough to tuck into the limo.

• • •

IT TOOK SEVEN YEARS to get *Splash* from ignition point to the Westwood Avco theater. I didn't just need an idea I felt passionately about—a good idea. I needed persistence. Determination.

Just like curiosity and storytelling reinforce each other, so do curiosity and persistence. Curiosity leads to storytelling, and storytelling inspires curiosity. The exact same dynamic works with curiosity and persistence.

Curiosity rewards persistence. If you get discouraged when you can't find the answer to a question immediately, if you give up with the first "no," then your curiosity isn't serving you very well. For me, that is one of the lessons of working with Anthea Sylbert—my persistence helped me stay the course, my curiosity helped me figure out how to change the mermaid movie just a little bit so other people understood it and appreciated it. There's nothing more fruitless and unhelpful than idle curiosity. Persistence is what carries curiosity to some worthwhile resolution.

Likewise, persistence without curiosity may mean you chase a goal that isn't worthy of the effort—or you chase a goal without adjusting as you learn new information. You end up way off course. Persistence is the drive moving you forward. Curiosity provides the navigation.

Curiosity can help spark a great idea, and help you refine it.

Determination can help you push the idea forward in the face of skepticism from others.

Together, they can give you confidence that you're onto something smart. And that confidence is the foundation of your ambition.

Asking questions is the key—to helping yourself, refining your ideas, persuading others. And that's true even if you think you know what you're doing and where you're heading.

I got the chance to turn one of the great Dr. Seuss books into a movie. I won the rights to *How the Grinch Stole Christmas!* from Dr. Seuss's widow, Audrey Geisel, in a two-year process competing with other great filmmakers who wanted the chance, including John Hughes (*Ferris Bueller's Day Off*, *Home Alone*), Tom Shadyac (who directed our movie *Liar Liar*), and the Farrelly brothers (*There's Something About Mary*).

In fact, *How the Grinch Stole Christmas!* would be the first Seuss book Audrey allowed to be turned into a full-length movie. Audrey Geisel was a little like Isaac Asimov's wife, in fact: she was a fierce protector of the legacy of her husband, who died in 1991. The California license plate on her car when we were working with her was a single word: "GRINCH." (Theodor Geisel also had the "GRINCH" license plate during the later years of his life.)[6]

I persuaded Jim Carrey to play the Grinch and persuaded Ron Howard to direct. Audrey Geisel insisted on meeting and talking to both of them in advance.

When I take on a project like turning *How the Grinch Stole Christmas!* into a movie, I feel a real sense of responsibility. The book was first published in 1957, and it has been a part of the childhood of essentially every American child born since then.

I was as familiar with the story, the characters, the art of *Grinch* as any other fifty-year-old adult in the United States. It was read to me as a child, and I'd read it to my own children.

But as we embarked on writing a script, on creating Whoville, and transferring the mood of the book to the screen, I kept a set of questions in mind—questions I asked myself, questions I asked Ron and Jim and the writers Jeff Price and Peter Seaman, over and over as we were making the movie.

We had won the rights; now the most important questions were: What, exactly, is this story? What kind of story is it?

Is it a verbal comedy?

Is it a physical comedy?

Is it an action picture?

Is it a myth?

The answer to each of these questions is "yes." That's what made it a challenge and a responsibility. When you were working on the physical comedy, you couldn't forget that you were also the keeper of a myth. When you were working on the action, you couldn't forget that the joy and the playfulness of the story come from Dr. Seuss's original language, as much as from anything he drew, or we designed.

Asking questions allows you to understand how other people are thinking about your idea. If Ron Howard thinks *Grinch* is an action picture and I think it's a verbal comedy, we've got a problem. The way to find out is to ask. Often the simplest questions are the best.

What kind of movie is *Grinch*?

What story are we telling?

What feeling are we trying to convey, especially when the audience is going to arrive with their own set of feelings about the story?

That too is at the heart of what good movie producers do.

You always want to create a movie that is original, that has passion. With a story as iconic as *Grinch*, you also need to keep the audience's expectations in mind. Everyone walking into a movie theater to see *How the Grinch Stole Christmas!* would already have a feeling about what they thought the story was.

And no one more vividly or more firmly than Audrey Geisel. She was our most challenging audience—our audience of one. We showed her the movie in the Hitchcock Theater on the Universal Studios lot. There were just five people in the room. Audrey sat very near the front. I sat thirty rows back from her, near the back, because I was so nervous about her reaction. A couple of editors and sound guys sat in the rows between us.

As the credits rolled, Audrey started clapping. She was beaming. She loved it. Sitting there in the screening room, I was so happy to have made her happy that I had tears streaming down my face.

Even a classic story, one that is totally familiar, can't succeed without the kind of elemental curiosity we brought to *Grinch*, so everyone agrees on the story you're trying to tell and the way you're trying to tell it.[7]

It seems so obvious. But how often have you been involved in a project where you get halfway along and discover that the people involved had slightly different understandings of what you were up to—differences that turned out to make it impossible to work effectively together, because everyone didn't actually agree on the goal?

It happens every day—in movies, in marketing, in architecture and advertising, in journalism and politics, and in the whole rest of the world. It even happens in sports. Nothing says miscommunication like a busted pass play in an NFL game.

It's a little counterintuitive, but rather than derailing or distracting you, questions can keep you on course.

Being determined in the face of obstacles is vital. Theodor Geisel, Dr. Seuss, is a great example of that himself. Many of his forty-four books remain wild bestsellers. In 2013, *Green Eggs and Ham* sold more than 700,000 copies in the United States (more than *Goodnight Moon*); *The Cat in the Hat* sold more than 500,000 copies, as did *Oh, the Places You'll Go!* and *One Fish Two Fish Red Fish Blue Fish*. And five more Dr. Seuss books each sold more than 250,000 copies. That's eight books, with total sales of more than 3.5 million copies, in one year (another eight Seuss titles sold 100,000 copies or more). Theodor Geisel is selling 11,000 Dr. Seuss books every day of the year, in the United States alone, twenty-four years after he died. He has sold 600 million books worldwide since his first book, *And to Think That I Saw It on Mulberry Street*, was published in 1937. And as inevitable as Dr. Seuss's appeal seems now, *Mulberry Street* was rejected by twenty-seven publishers before being accepted by Vanguard Press. What if Geisel had decided that twenty rejections were enough for him? Or twenty-five?

Imagine childhood, and reading, without Dr. Seuss.[8]

I feel like we enter the world, newborn, and at that moment, the answer is "yes." And it's "yes" for a little while after that. The world is openhearted to us. But at some point, the world starts saying "no," and the sooner you start practicing ways of getting around "no," the better. I now think of myself as impervious to rejection.

We've been talking about using curiosity when the world says "no." But just as often, the "no" can come from inside your head, and curiosity can be the cure to that kind of "no" too.

As I mentioned earlier, when I have a fear of something, I try to get curious about it—I try to set the fear aside long enough to start asking questions. The questions do two things: they distract me from the queasy feeling, and I learn something about what I'm worried about. Instinctively, I think, we all know that. But sometimes you need to remind yourself that the best way to dispel the fear is to face it, to be curious.

I am a nervous public speaker. I give a good speech, but I don't enjoy getting ready to give a speech, I don't even necessarily enjoy giving the speech—what I enjoy is having given it. The fun part is talking to people about the speech after it's done.

For me, every time I do it is a test. Here's how I keep the nervousness at bay:

First, I don't start preparing too far in advance, because for me, that just opens up the box of worry. If I start writing the speech two weeks in advance, then I just worry every day for two weeks.

So I make sure I have enough time to prepare, and I start working on the talk a few days before I have to give it.

I do the same thing I did with *Grinch*. I ask questions:

What's the talk supposed to be about?

What's the best possible version of the talk?

What do the people coming to this event expect to hear?

What do they want to hear, in general?

What do they want to hear from me, specifically?

And who is the audience?

The answer to each of those questions helps me create a framework for what I'm supposed to talk about. And the answers immediately spark ideas, anecdotes, and points I want to make—which I keep track of.

I'm always looking for stories to tell—stories that make the points I want to make. In terms of giving a speech, I'm looking for stories for two reasons. People like stories—they don't want to be lectured, they want to be entertained. And I know the stories I'm telling—so even if I stumble or lose my way, well, it's my story. I can't actually forget what I'm trying to say. I won't be thrown off stride.

In the end, I write out the whole speech a day or two in advance. And I practice several times.

Writing the speech gets it into my brain.

Practicing also gets it into my brain—and practicing shows me the rough spots, or the spots where the point and the story don't fit perfectly, or where I'm not sure I'm telling the joke exactly right. Practicing gives me a chance to edit—just like you edit a movie, or a magazine story, or a business presentation, or a book.

I bring the full text of the speech with me, I set it on the podium, and then I stand next to the podium and talk. I don't read the speech from the pages. I have the text in case I need it. But I don't usually need it.

Does curiosity require work?

Of course it does.

Even if you're "naturally curious"—whatever that phrase means to you—asking questions, absorbing the answers, figuring out in what direction the answers point you, figuring out what other questions you need to ask, that's all work.

I do think of myself as naturally curious, but I've also exercised my curiosity in all kinds of situations, all day long, for almost sixty years. Sometimes you have to remember to use curiosity—you have to remind yourself to use it. If someone's telling you "no," that can easily throw you off stride. You can get so caught up in being rejected, in not getting something you're working toward, that you forget to ask questions about what's happening. Why am I being told no?

If you have a fear of giving a speech, you can become so distracted or put off that you avoid it instead of plunging in. That prolongs the anxiety, and it doesn't help the speech, it hurts it. The speech doesn't write itself, and the way to manage being nervous about the speech is to work on it.

I have found that using curiosity to get around the "no," whether "no" is coming from someone else or from my own brain, has taught me some other valuable ways of confronting resistance, of getting things done.

A great piece of advice came to me from my longtime friend Herbert A. Allen, the investment banker and creator of the remarkable media and technology conference he hosts every year in Sun Valley, Idaho (called simply the Allen & Co. Sun Valley Conference).

Many years ago, he told me: make the hardest call of the day first.

The hardest call of the day might be someone you fear is going to give you bad news. The hardest call might be someone to whom you have to deliver bad news. The hardest call might be someone you want to see in person who might be avoiding you.

And Allen was being metaphoric. The "hardest call" might be an email you have to send, it might be a conversation you need to have in person with someone in your own office.

Whatever it is, the reason you think of it as the "hardest call of the day" is because there's something scary about it. It's going to be uncomfortable in some way—either in the encounter itself, or in the outcome of the encounter. But Allen's point is that a task like that isn't going to be less scary at noon or at 4:30 in the afternoon. Just the opposite, the low-grade anxiety from "the hardest call" is going to cast a shadow over the whole day. It's going to distract you, maybe even make you less effective. It will certainly make you less openhearted.

"Make the hardest call first." That's not quite about curiosity, and it's not quite about determination—it's a little bit of both. It's grit. It's character. Grab hold of the one task that really must be done—however much you're not looking forward to it—and tackle it.

That clears the air. It brightens the rest of the day. It may, in fact, reset the agenda for part of the day. It gives you confidence to tackle whatever else is coming—because you've done the hardest thing first. And while the outcome of "the hardest call" usually goes just like you imagine, sometimes there's a surprise there too.

Asking questions always seems, superficially, like an admission of ignorance. How can admitting your ignorance be the path to confidence?

That's one of the many wonderful dualities of curiosity.

Curiosity helps you dispel ignorance and confusion, curiosity evaporates fogginess and uncertainty, it clears up disagreement.

Curiosity can give you confidence. And the confidence can give you determination. And the confidence and determination can give you ambition. That's how you get beyond the "no," whether it's coming from other people, or from inside your own mind.

If you harness curiosity to your dreams, it can help power them along to reality.

.   .   .

ABOUT A DECADE AGO, the New York style magazine *W* did a profile of me with the headline:

THE MOGUL

Brian Grazer, whose movies have grossed $10.5 billion, is arguably the most successful producer in town—and surely the most recognizable.

Is it the hair?[9]

People in Hollywood, of course, know the hair.

People in the rest of the world—people who may not even know my name but know *A Beautiful Mind* or *Arrested Development* or *The Da Vinci Code*—some of them know the hair too. "That Hollywood guy with the hair that stands straight up"— that's a common description of me.

The hair is part of my image, part of my persona.

And the hair is no accident. Of course it isn't an accident— because I have to gel it vertical every single morning.

But my hair isn't just a fashion quirk. It's not even really a matter of personal taste.

After Ron Howard and I had done a couple of movies, I was building a reasonable reputation in Hollywood. It was nothing like the visibility of Ron, of course—he was a star and a director and the icon of an era. I was a producer, and also a newcomer, especially compared to Ron.

But I wanted to make an impression. Hollywood is a land of style, a world where how you present yourself matters. Many of the people working here are so dramatically good-looking, that is their style. That's not me, and I know that.

When Ron and I were getting Imagine up and running in

the early nineties, it was during a period when male Holly-wood producers were developing a kind of collective persona. There was a group of young, successful producers doing loud, aggressive movies. They were themselves loud and aggressive—they were "yellers," people who sometimes managed their col-leagues by throwing things and screaming. And many in this same group wore beards. Bearded, aggressive men, producing aggressive movies.

That wasn't me. I wasn't doing loud movies, I don't look great with facial hair. I worked for a couple of screamers in my early days in Hollywood. I don't like being screamed at, and I am not a screamer myself.

But I didn't want to simply fade into the background. I felt I needed to define myself in a way that made me memorable.

So this question of personal style—what to wear, how to look—was on my mind.

It all fell into place one afternoon in 1993, when I was swimming with my daughter Sage, who was then about five. As I surfaced in the pool, I ran my fingers through my wet hair, standing it straight up.

"That looks cool!" Sage said.

I looked at myself in the mirror with my hair standing up, and I thought, "That's really interesting."

So I gelled it straight up. I started that very day.

The hair got noticed. It instantly produced an extreme reac-tion from people.

I'd say 25 percent of people thought it was cool.

Another 50 percent of people were curious about it. Why do you do your hair like that? How do you do your hair like that?

Some people who already knew me were in this curious category. They said, Brian, what's up with the hair? What are you thinking? What got you to do that?

Then there was the other 25 percent—the people who hated the hair. The hair made them angry. They looked at my hair and immediately decided I was an asshole.

I loved that. I really liked getting that extreme range of reactions from people. The hair inspired curiosity about me. Right after I started wearing my hair up, I would sometimes hear people talking about it when they thought I couldn't hear them.

"Hey, what's with Grazer? What's he doing with his hair?"

Michael Ovitz, the famous superagent and Hollywood power broker, grew up in the business right alongside me. He lobbied me. "Don't do the hair," Michael said. "Business people won't take you seriously."

Some people thought I was arrogant because of the hair.

The truth is that it had occurred to me that the world of Hollywood is divided into two categories—business folks and artists. I thought this hairstyle tipped me over into the artist category, where I was more comfortable.

After having my hair straight up for a few months, I did think about stopping. So many people seemed to be talking about it.

But then I realized something: yes, the hair was inspiring curiosity about me, but what was really interesting was that people's reactions to the hair said more about what they thought of me than they revealed about me, or my hair.

I came to see my hair as a test to the world. I felt like I was eliciting the truth about how people felt about me much more quickly than having to wait for it to come out. So I left it up.

In a way, the hair does something else for me. It lets people know that this guy isn't quite what he seems. He's a little unpredictable. I'm not a prepackaged, shrink-wrapped guy. I'm a little different.

Here's why my hair is important.

Hollywood and show business really are a small town, and as in any industry, there is a pretty defined system of rules and practices and traditions. To get things done, you have to follow the rules.

Mind you, all I did was gel my hair straight up, just as a gambit, and some people went completely crazy about it. Not just some people—one out of four people.

My hair doesn't have the slightest impact on any script or director or talent, it doesn't change the marketing of a movie or the opening weekend grosses. But it made a lot of people—some of them important people—really uncomfortable.

Now imagine the reaction, the resistance, when you do something different in a category where it really matters.

But I don't want to do the same kind of work everyone's doing. I don't even want to do the same kind of work I was doing ten years ago or five years ago.

I want variety. I want to tell new stories—or classic stories in new ways—both because that makes my life interesting, and because it makes going to the movie theater or turning on the TV interesting.

I want the opportunity to be different.

Where do I get the confidence to be different?

A lot of it comes from curiosity. I spent years as a young man trying to understand the business I'm in. I have spent decades staying connected to how the rest of the world works.

The curiosity conversations give me a reservoir of experience and insight that goes well beyond my own firsthand experience.

But the conversations also give me a lot of firsthand experience in exposing my own lack of knowledge, my own naïveté. I actually practice being a little ignorant. I'm willing to admit what I don't know, because I know that's how I get smarter. Asking questions may seem to expose your ignorance, but what it really does is just the opposite. People who ask questions, in fact, are rarely thought of as stupid.

The epigram that opens this chapter—"Curiosity will conquer fear even more than bravery will"—comes from a book by the Irish poet James Stephens. The quote goes on a little longer and makes a central point:

> Curiosity will conquer fear even more than bravery will; indeed, it has led many people into dangers which mere physical courage would shudder away from, for hunger and love and curiosity are the great impelling forces of life.

That's what curiosity has done for me, and what I think it can do for almost anyone. It can give you the courage to be adventurous and ambitious. It does that by getting you comfortable with being a little uncomfortable. The start of any journey is always a little nerve-racking.

I have learned to surf as an adult. I have learned to paint as an adult. I learned to surf much better after producing *Blue Crush*, a female-empowerment movie that we shot on the north shore of Oahu. Some of the people working on the movie were surfing there—surfing some of the biggest waves in the world—and I became fascinated with how waves work and what it was like to ride them. I love surfing—it requires so much concentration, it wipes away completely the concerns of the moment. It's also totally thrilling.

I love painting in much the same way. I find it utterly relaxing. I'm not a great painter, I'm not even a particularly good painter in technical terms. But I figured out that a lot of what matters in painting is what you're trying to say, not whether you say it perfectly. I don't need to have great painting technique to find real originality in it, and to be energized by it. I learned to paint after meeting Andy Warhol and Roy Lichtenstein.

In both cases, my curiosity conquered my fear. I was inspired to do both those things by some of the people who did them best in the world. I wasn't trying to be a world-class surfer or a world-class painter. I was just curious to taste the joy, the thrill, the satisfaction that those people got from mastering something that is both hard and rewarding.

Curiosity gives you power. It's not the kind of power that comes from yelling and being aggressive. It's a quiet kind of power. It's a cumulative power. Curiosity is power for real people, it's power for people who don't have superpowers.

So I protect that part of myself—the part that's not afraid to seem briefly ignorant. Not knowing the answer opens up the world, as long as you don't try to hide what you don't know. I try never to be self-conscious about not knowing.

As it turns out, the people who hated my hair back in the beginning were right. It is a little bit of a challenge. The hair looks like just a matter of personal style—but for me, it is a way of reminding myself every day that I am trying to be a little different, that it's okay to be a little different, that being different requires courage, just like gelling your hair straight up requires courage, but you can be different in ways that make most people smile.

I gel my hair every morning first thing when I wake up. It takes about ten seconds. I never skip the gel. And twenty years after I started doing it, it has become my signature—and my approach to work matches my hair. It's also still a great way of starting a conversation and standing out.

In February 2001, I got to spend four days in Cuba with a group of seven friends who are also media executives. The group included Graydon Carter, the editor of *Vanity Fair*; Tom Freston, then CEO of MTV; Bill Roedy, then president of MTV; producer Brad Grey; Jim Wiatt, then chief of the talent agency William Morris; and Les Moonves, who is president of CBS.[10]

As part of the visit, we had a long lunch with Fidel Castro. Castro was wearing his usual green army fatigues, and he talked to us through a translator for three and a half hours—I think without even taking a breath. It was the usual Castro speech, mostly about why Cuba is amazing and the United States is doomed.

When he stopped talking, he looked at me—I wasn't necessarily the most prominent person in the group—and through the translator he asked just one question: "How do you get your hair to stand up that way?" Everybody laughed.

Even Castro loved the hair.

CHAPTER FIVE

Every Conversation Is a Curiosity Conversation

"Connection gives meaning to our lives. Connection is why we're here."

—Brené Brown[1]

IN THE SPRING OF 1995, we at Imagine Entertainment got a new boss. Like anyone, I wanted to make a good impression. I just wasn't quite sure how to do that.

In fact, I haven't had a boss in the conventional sense in thirty years, someone who could call me up and tell me what to do, someone I had to check in with every few days. Ron Howard and I had been running Imagine together—along with a lot of other people—since 1986.

During that time, we've had our longest partnership with Universal Studios—they finance and distribute many of the movies we produce. So I consider whoever is running Universal my "boss" in the sense that we need to work well with that person, we need to develop and sustain a strong personal and professional relationship so we can agree on the kinds of movies we're making together. Tens of millions of dollars are always hanging in the balance.

By the mid-1990s, we'd done a run of movies with Universal that were both great and successful: *Parenthood* (1989), *Kindergarten Cop* (1990), *Backdraft* (1991), and *The Paper* (1994).

When Lew Wasserman was running Universal, I wanted to know Lew—beyond my youthful encounter where he gave me the pencil and the legal pad.

When the Japanese electronics company Matsushita bought Universal, I got to know Matsushita executive Tsuzo Murase.

And when Matsushita sold Universal to the Seagram Company in 1995—yes, Universal Studios went from being independent, to being owned by a Japanese electronics company, to being owned by a Canadian liquor company—I wanted to know Seagram's CEO Edgar Bronfman, Jr.

I didn't hear from Bronfman during the first few weeks after the deal was announced. I did hear that Bronfman had called Steven Spielberg and director and producer Ivan Reitman. So I wondered what to do.

I was a movie producer, producing lots of movies with what had suddenly become Bronfman's company.

Edgar Bronfman was the CEO of a company then doing $6.4 billion in business a year. I wasn't quite sure how to reach out.

Should I call his office?

Should I send an email?

Bob Iger, the CEO of Disney, is a close friend who once gave me a piece of advice that has stuck with me. In the right circumstances, he said, "Doing nothing can be a very powerful action unto itself."

Iger has years of experience in high-risk, high-pressure situations. These days, in the space of seventy-two hours, he can be in Moscow with Vladimir Putin, then in London on the set of the new *Star Wars* movie, then in China working at Shanghai Disney, and then back home in Los Angeles at one of his kids' basketball games. That same weekend, he can return eager to talk about the eighteen-hundred-page biography of Winston Churchill that he finished reading during all his travels. Bob's insistence on excellence, and his own wide-ranging curiosity, are tireless.

As I was thinking about how to approach Bronfman, Bob's advice occurred to me. I tend to think that *action* is the way to get action on something. I know how to be patient, but I don't usually leave things alone. I nudge them along. At least, that's how I operated in the first years of my career. This time I decided to wait. To take no action.

"Doing nothing can be a very powerful action unto itself."

Then the White House called, and solved the problem for me.

That spring we were getting ready to release *Apollo 13* for a summer premiere—it was set to open June 30, 1995, in 2,200 theaters. In May, we got a call from the White House, inviting us to show the movie to President Bill Clinton, his family, and guests three weeks before it was released, on June 8, in the White House screening room.

That's how a White House movie screening works—the movie itself is invited to the White House, and all the people responsible for making it get to come along.

So Tom Hanks was going to the *Apollo 13* screening at the White House, along with his wife, Rita Wilson, and so was the NASA astronaut that Hanks portrayed, Jim Lovell. The film's director, Ron Howard, was going, and as the producer, I was going too. Also invited: Ron Meyer, the head of Universal Studios, and Edgar Bronfman, the CEO of the company that owned Universal.

What could be more perfect?

My movie gets invited to the White House—perhaps the most prestigious single movie screen in the whole country. And my new boss at Universal gets to be a guest at the White House, not just to see my movie, but *because* of my movie.

That's about as great an introduction to the boss as you could want.

It was my first time at the White House. The night started with a cocktail reception. Bronfman was there. President Clinton and Hillary joined us (Chelsea didn't), some senators and congressmen, a cabinet secretary or two.

After the cocktails, we all stepped into the White House screening room, which is surprisingly small, just sixty seats. They served popcorn; it was very homey, not fancy at all.

President Clinton sat through the whole movie. And as it ended, at the moment when NASA Mission Control reestablished radio contact with the returning Apollo capsule, as the familiar trio of orange-and-white parachutes popped out on the TV screens in Mission Control, the screening room burst into applause.

It was, as I expected, a great setting to meet Edgar Bronfman. A lot of people were competing for his attention that night, of course, but we talked for a few minutes. Bronfman, tall and lanky, is very elegant, and extremely well mannered. "I love this movie," he told me. "I'm so proud of this."

He was just a few weeks into owning Universal, but you could tell how genuinely excited he was about the movie business. He came out to Los Angeles three weeks later for the official premiere of *Apollo 13* with his wife, Clarissa. The White House screening was the start of a friendship, and a working relationship, that lasted through the five years that Edgar owned and ran Universal as part of Seagram.

It was my first time meeting President Clinton, and as so many other people have related from their experience, President Clinton seemed to make a point of connecting with me—a connection that continues to this day. President Clinton clearly appreciated the spirit of *Apollo 13*, the way the movie captures the NASA engineers and astronauts turning a potential disaster into a triumph of American ingenuity.

President Clinton later became a big fan of the TV show *24*, which premiered after his second term ended. From his perspective, he told me, *24* had a special emotional punch. He said the show captured a lot of the details of intelligence and counterterrorism work accurately—and that in the end, Jack Bauer always nails the bad guy. In real life, he told me, the president and the country's intelligence and defense staff are often tangled in bureaucracy and legal limitations and red tape, not to mention uncertainty. For President Clinton, *24* is a wish-fulfillment experience: sometimes, he said, it would have been nice to move with the boldness and independence of Jack Bauer.

. . .

IN WRITING ABOUT CURIOSITY so far, I've tried to tease apart the kinds of curiosity—we've tried to granularize it, to create a taxonomy of thinking about, classifying, and using it.

As a tool for discovery, as a kind of secret weapon to understand what other people don't.

As a spark for creativity and inspiration.

As a way of motivating yourself.

As a tool for independence and self-confidence.

As the key to storytelling.

As a form of courage.

But I think the most valuable use of curiosity is one we haven't explored yet. In fact, I had only recently stumbled into this quality of curiosity—or at least, stumbled into recognizing it. It's so obvious that when I say it, you may briefly roll your eyes. But it's also hidden: it's a kind of curiosity that we neglect and overlook more than the others, even though it has the most power to improve our lives, the lives of those closest to us, and the lives of those we work with every day. I'm talking about the human connection that is created by curiosity.

Human connection is the most important element of our daily lives—with our colleagues and bosses, our romantic partners, our children, our friends.

Human connection requires sincerity. It requires compassion. It requires trust.

Can you really have sincerity, or compassion, or trust, without curiosity?

I don't think so. I think when you stop to consider it—when you look at your own experiences at work and at home—what's so clear is that authentic human connection requires curiosity.

To be a good boss, you have to be curious about the people who work for you. And to be a good colleague, a good romantic partner, a good parent, you have to be curious as well.

True love requires curiosity, and sustaining that love requires sustaining your curiosity. Real intimacy requires curiosity.

I use curiosity every day to help manage people at work, not just in all the ways we've talked about, but as a tool to build trust and cooperation and engagement.

I use curiosity every day with my fiancée and my kids and

my friends—not always as skillfully as I would like, I confess—but I use curiosity to keep my relationships vital and fresh, to keep connected.

Human connection is the most important part of being alive. It's the key to sustained happiness and to a sense of satisfaction with how you're living.

And curiosity is the key to connecting and staying connected.

I had a meeting on the couches in my office not too long ago with one of my movie production executives.

She had come in to talk about the state of a movie we're working on, with a cast of big-name movie stars, and a series of intertwining stories.

The meeting was short, really just a progress report. Many movies bump and grind along for a lot of months, and a lot of meetings, before either landing on the theater screen, or running out of energy and simply never getting made.

This particular movie had been in the works for more than a year already, but not a scene had been shot.

I listened to the update for a few minutes before gently interrupting. "Why should we do this movie?" I asked. "Why *are* we doing this movie?"

My colleague stopped and looked at me. She'd been at Imagine a long time and knew me pretty well. She answered my question by simply reciting how we got into this movie, in brisk shorthand—who brought it to us, why it was exciting at that moment.

I knew all that. And she knew I knew it. She was answering the question of why we *were* doing this movie, but she wasn't answering the question of why we *should* do this movie.

A few minutes later, I tried again.

"Do you love this movie?" I asked.

She smiled. She didn't shake her head, but she might as well have. Without saying a word, her smile said: *Do I love this movie? What kind of question is that? I love the idea of getting this movie made after all these meetings, all these negotiations, all these changes in cast and schedule—that's what I love.*

She slipped my question like a boxer side-stepping a punch. Love? What's love? This movie is in the ditch at the moment. We loved it once: loved the idea, loved the cast, loved the package, loved the mood we were going to create for the Friday night movie crowds . . . a year ago. Now the movie just needed to be winched out of the ditch. Who knew whether we loved it anymore? We couldn't possibly love it until we saw some of it on a screen.

I just nodded.

My colleague ticked off a couple of other things—she is well organized and typically comes to my office with a list of the things she needs to make sure we talk about. When she was done with her list, she whisked off.

I hadn't told her what to do about the stalled movie.

And she hadn't asked what to do about the stalled movie.

But she very clearly knew how I felt about it. I didn't love it anymore. I couldn't really remember loving it that much. I thought it had become a burden, taking time and energy and emotion we should have been putting into projects we really did love.

But here's a key element of my personality: I don't like to boss people around. I don't get motivated by telling people what to do, I don't take any pleasure in it.

So I manage with curiosity by asking questions.

I actually do it instinctively now. I don't need to stop and remind myself to ask questions instead of giving instructions. Work these days for many people is filled with one meeting or conversation or conference call after another. In a typical day, I may have fifty conversations of some substance. But I so prefer hearing what other people have to say, that I instinctively ask questions. If you're listening to my side of a phone call, you may hear little but the occasional question.

My sense is that most managers and bosses, and most workplaces, don't work that way.

Sometimes you have to give orders.

Sometimes I have to give orders.

But if you set aside the routine instructions that are part of everyone's workday—the request to get someone on the phone, to look up a fact, to schedule a meeting—I almost always start with questions.

I especially think questions are a great management tool when I think someone isn't doing what I would hope they would, or when I think something isn't going in the direction I want it to go.

People often imagine that if there's going to be conflict, they need to start with a firm hand, they need to remind people of the chain of command.

I'm never worried about who is in charge.

I'm worried about making sure we get the best possible decision, the best possible casting, script, movie trailer, financing deal, the best possible movie.

Asking questions elicits information, of course.

Asking questions creates the space for people to raise issues they are worried about that the boss, or their colleagues, may not know about.

Asking questions gives people the chance to tell a different story than the one you're expecting.

Most important from my perspective is asking questions means people have to make their case for the way they want a decision to go.

The movie business is all about being able to "make your case." With *Splash*, I had to make my case hundreds of times over seven years. After thirty years of successfully making movies, that hasn't changed for me. In the summer of 2014, we produced the movie *Get On Up*, the story of James Brown and his monumental impact on the music we listen to every day. Tate Taylor, who directed *The Help*, directed the film. Mick Jagger coproduced. Chad Boseman, who played Jackie Robinson in the movie *42*, starred as James Brown.

I worked for years to make a movie about James Brown and his music. His story is so elemental, so American. It wasn't just that James Brown came from poverty, that he cut through discrimination—his childhood was devastating, he was abandoned by both his mother and his father and raised in a brothel. He didn't have much basic education, and no formal musical education. And yet he created a whole new sound in music, a sound that is irresistible. He created a whole new way of performing on stage. James Brown had to be totally self-reliant, totally self-created. His impact on American music is profound. But he paid a huge price. His is a story about finding identity and self-worth. It's a story of great triumph and also sadness, for him and for those closest to him.

I'd been interested in James Brown's music and his life for twenty years. I worked with James Brown himself on doing a movie for eight years—buying the rights to his life, trying to get the story and the script right, meeting with him over and over. But when he died in 2006 before we had gotten a movie made, the rights to his story reverted to his estate. I was discouraged. We had to start all over.

I knew Mick Jagger, the lead singer of the Rolling Stones, a little bit—I'd met him several times. Mick was as passionate about the power of James Brown's music and story as I was. After Brown died, Mick called me up. "Let's make this movie together," he said. He knew I had a working script. He said he would try to renegotiate the rights.

And then we had to go make the case, again, to Universal Pictures—which had already lost money during my first round trying to get a James Brown movie made.

Mick and I went to see Donna Langley, the head of Universal Pictures. She's English and grew up adoring the Rolling Stones. It was a fantastic meeting. Mick is so graceful, so relaxed, so eloquent. He talked to Donna about James Brown, about the script, about the kind of movie we wanted to make. All in that classic Mick Jagger accent. He made it fun. He made it appealing.

And it worked. Still, after I'd been in the movie business thirty-five years, after I'd won an Oscar, putting *Get On Up* on the screen took sixteen years—and I needed Mick Jagger's help to make it happen.

So if you're going to survive in Hollywood—and I think if you're going to survive and thrive anywhere in business—you have to learn to "make the case" for whatever you want to do. Making the case means answering the big questions: Why this project? Why now? Why with this group of talent? With this investment of money? Who is the audience (or the customer)? How will we capture that audience, that customer?

And the biggest question of all—the question I'm always pulling back to the center of the conversation: What's the story? What's this movie about?

Making the case also means answering the detail questions: Why these songs in that order on the soundtrack? Why that supporting actress? Why that scene?

None of these are yes-or-no questions. They are open-ended questions—they are questions where the answer can itself be a story, sometimes short, sometimes a longer one.

I ask these questions, and I listen to the answers. Sometimes I listen with a skeptical expression on my face, I'm sure. Sometimes I listen with a distracted look in my eye.

And sometimes you need to ask questions that are even more open.

What are you focused on?

Why are you focused on that?

What are you worried about?

What's your plan?

I think asking questions creates a lot more engagement in the people with whom you work. It's subtle. Let's say you have a movie that's in trouble. You ask the executive responsible for moving that movie along what her plan is. You're doing two things just by asking the question. You're making it clear that she should have a plan, and you're making it clear that she is in charge of that plan. The question itself implies both the responsibility for the problem and the authority to come up with the solution.

If you work with talented people who want to do the work they are doing, then they'll want to step up. But it's a simple quality of human nature that people prefer to choose to do things rather than be ordered to do them. In fact, as soon as you tell me I have to do something—give a speech, attend a banquet, go to Cannes—I immediately start looking for ways to avoid doing it. If you invite me to do something, I'm much more likely to want to do it.

I work every day with actors, with beautiful, charming, charismatic people whose job is to persuade you to believe them. That's what being a great actor means—it means having the ability to cast a spell over the audience, to persuade them you are the character you're portraying. A great actor creates believability.

But if you pause for a moment and think about it, you'll realize that employing people like that is really hard. Actors are hard to manage because they are often used to getting what they want, and because their talent is persuading you to see the world the way they want you to. That's why you've hired them in the first place.

Am I the "boss" of the movie? Is the director the "boss" of the movie? In different ways, of course, the producer and the director are the "bosses" of the movie.

When you're out on location, you can be spending $300,000 a day to make a movie. That's $12,500 an hour, even while everyone is sleeping.

So if an actor gets mad, or pouty, or wants their jet refueled, they are the person shaking the cage. They are the person in charge.

You can't let people behave badly. But you also can't screw up the psyche of an actor. If someone ends up with a bad attitude, you don't get the performance you want.

When there's a problem, when there's trouble at $300,000 a day, you want to find a way to have a conversation so that you can convince your star or stars to help you. You want to draw them in, not order them around.

Back in 1991, we shot the movie *Far and Away*. We had

Tom Cruise as the lead. Tom was at the top of his career. He was only twenty-nine years old, but he had already made *Top Gun* (1986), *The Color of Money* (1986), *Rain Man* (1988), and *Born on the Fourth of July* (1989).

Tom isn't difficult to work with. But *Far and Away* was a challenging movie to get made. It was an old-fashioned epic, a story of two immigrants leaving Ireland for America at the turn of the last century. We shot in Ireland and the western United States. It got expensive, but it wasn't overtly commercial. When we figured out what it was going to cost, the studio told me to find ways of cutting the budget.

I went to Tom on the set. We talked. I said, "Look, you're not the producer of this movie. But we all want to make it, we all have this vision of a movie we're doing as artists, a story we care about. It's going to be expensive, but we can't spend as much money as it looks like we're going to. We need to hold the line."

I said to Tom, "Can you be the team leader here with the cast and crew? Can you be the guy that sets an example?"

He looked at me and said, "I'm one hundred percent that guy!"

He said, "When I have to go to the bathroom, I'm going to run to the trailer and run back to the set. I'm going to set the pace for excellence, and respect, and tightening up."

And that's exactly what he did. He led. He was motivated. And he motivated other people.

I didn't walk in and tell Tom what to do. I didn't order everybody to work harder, to make do with less. I explained where we were. And I went to the key player, the person other people would respect, and I asked that person a question: "Can you be the leader here?"

Being persuasive, being successful, in a situation like that is hardly guaranteed. Some of it is in how you present yourself. I think Tom appreciated that I came to him with a problem, that I treated him as an equal, that I treated him as part of the solution. I allowed Tom to be curious about both the problem and how to fix it.

Some of that is Tom's character—he isn't just thinking of himself.

But you have a much greater chance of success at a key moment like that if you ask someone to step up in a big way, rather than order them to step up in a big way. Tom did it.

I think asking for people's help—rather than directing it— is almost always the smart way of doing things, regardless of the stakes.

For instance, I think my partnership with Ron Howard only works because we never tell each other what to do. We always ask.

If I need Ron to call Russell Crowe, I don't say, "Ron, I need you to call Russell Crowe." I say something like:

"How would you feel about calling Russell Crowe?"

Or, "Do you think it's a good idea if you call Russell Crowe?"

Or, "How do you think Russell Crowe would feel if you called him?"

Unless Ron asks me a specific yes-or-no question, I never tell him what to do.

The same is true of my relationship with Tom Hanks. Tom Cruise. Denzel Washington. I don't tell, I ask.

I am, of course, communicating what I want. But I'm leaving them the choice. They know what I want, but they have free will. They can say no.

This isn't just a matter of personal style. The real benefit of asking rather than telling is that it creates the space for a conversation, for a different idea, a different strategy.

I trust Ron Howard completely—I trust his artistic instincts, I trust his business judgment, I trust his affection and respect for me and for what we've created.

So I don't want to say, "Ron, I need you to call Russell Crowe."

I want to say, "Ron, what would happen if you called Russell Crowe?" Because then Ron can wrinkle his brow, and come up with a different way of approaching Russell with whatever idea we've got.

I've discovered another unexpected characteristic of using questions: they transmit values. In fact, questions can quietly transmit values more powerfully than a direct statement telling people what you want them to stand for, or exhorting them about what you want them to stand for.

Why do I ask my movie production executive if she loves that movie that isn't moving along? Because I want her to love the movies she's making for us. We've been doing this business for a long time, and at this point the only reason to do a project is because we love it. If I say to her, or anyone else: "Let's only do movies you really love," it's easy for that to sound like a goal, or a theory, or, worst of all, a platitude.

If I ask directly, "Do you love this movie?"—the question makes it clear what I think our priorities really are.

It worked exactly the same way with Tom Cruise and *Far and Away*. If I fly to Ireland from Los Angeles and start telling everybody that we need to save money, we need to film faster, cut effects, save costs on the catering—well then I'm just the LA executive who flies in with the bad news and the marching orders.

If I sit down quietly with Tom and ask the question, "Can you be the leader here?"—it's a moment packed with values. We care about this movie. We've got to find a way of protecting the integrity of the story while living within a reasonable budget. I need help. And I have so much respect for Tom that I'm asking him to help me solve this problem, to help me manage the whole movie. This is a powerful message, packed into only six words, with a question mark at the end instead of a period.

. . .

CURIOSITY AT WORK ISN'T a matter of style. It's much more consequential than that.

If you're the boss, and you manage by asking questions, you're laying the foundation for the culture of your company or your group.

You're letting people know that the boss is willing to listen. This isn't about being "warm" or "friendly." It's about understanding how complicated the modern business world is, how indispensable diversity of perspective is, and how hard creative work is.

Here's why it's hard: because often there is no right answer.

Consider for a moment an example that seems really simple: the design of Google's search page.

How many ways are there to design a web page? How many ways are there to design a page for searching the web? An infinite number, of course.

Google's page is legendary for its spare, almost stark appearance. There's a clean page, a search box, a Google logo, two search buttons: "Google search" and "I'm feeling lucky." And wide open white space. Today, the Google home page is considered a triumph of graphic design, a brilliant example of taking something as complex and chaotic as the World Wide Web and making it simple and accessible. (Both Bing and Twitter seem to try to channel Google's simplicity and drama on their home pages—but neither can resist cluttering up the look.)

Two things are fascinating from the story of the design of Google's search page. First, it's an accident. Sergey Brin, one of Google's two cofounders, didn't know how to do HTML computer code when he and Larry Page first launched the search engine in 1998, so he designed the simplest possible page— because that's all he had the skills to do.

Second, people found the simple page so different from the rest of the cluttered web that they didn't understand what to do. People routinely sat in front of the clean page waiting for the rest of it to load instead of typing in their search. Google solved that confusion by putting a tiny copyright line at the bottom of the search page (it's not there anymore), so users would know the page had finished loading.[2]

So the story of Google's brilliant home page is surprising mostly because it wasn't done by design, and its brilliance took a while to become clear. Brin didn't know how to code anything fancy, so he didn't. And what has now become an influential example of online design usability was so baffling when it was first unveiled that people couldn't figure out how to use it.

But the home page isn't really Google at all. Google is the vast array of computer code and algorithms that allow the company to search the web and present those results. There are millions of lines of code behind a Google search—and millions more behind Google mail, Google Chrome, Google ads.

If we can envision dozens, hundreds of ways of designing a search page, imagine for a moment the ways that all that computer code could be written. It's like imagining the ways a book can be written, like imagining the ways a story could be told on screen. For Google, it is a story, just written in zeroes and ones.

That's why asking questions at work, instead of giving orders, is so valuable. Because most modern problems—lowering someone's cholesterol, getting passengers onto an airplane efficiently, or searching all of human knowledge—don't have a right answer. They have all kinds of answers, many of them wonderful.

To get at the possibilities, you have to find out what ideas and reactions are in other people's minds. You have to ask them questions.

How do you see this problem?

What are we missing?

Is there another way of tackling this?

How would we solve this if we were the customer?

That's as true in movies as in any other business. I love the movies we've made. But we didn't produce the "right" version of the iconic films *Apollo 13* or *A Beautiful Mind*. We have the version of the story that we made—the very best version, with the cast and crew and script and budget we had.

Tom Hanks is the face of *Apollo 13*, as real-life astronaut Jim Lovell.

Russell Crowe captures the spirit, the struggles, and the interior intellectual life of mathematician John Nash in *A Beautiful Mind*.

They both executed those roles brilliantly.

But clearly that isn't the only version of those movies that could have been made—what if we hadn't been able to sign Hanks or Crowe for those leading roles? We would have hired another actor. And the whole movie would have been different—even if every other actor, every other behind-the-scenes person, and every word of the script had been identical.

Anna Culp, who is senior vice president for movie production at Imagine, has been at the company sixteen years, having started as my assistant.

"We do approach everything as 'case-building,'" Anna says about the culture at Imagine. "Being asked questions means you always have the chance to make the movie better, and to make the case for making the movie better.

"For me, the questions mean no one is ever wrong. Most of the time, these aren't those kinds of right-or-wrong decisions.

"The movies we end up loving, you can't really imagine them having come out any other way. But with something like the James Brown movie, *Get On Up*, well, over sixteen years, at different times, there have been very different versions of that movie.

"For me, questions have become a habit I use myself. I'm always asking, 'Why am I doing this material, this movie?'

"And you know, if something doesn't work out financially— if it's not a success, you want to be able to stand back and say, 'This is still something I'm proud of.'

"The disadvantages of the questions are, in some sense, the same as the advantages. You wonder if you are delivering, and if you are delivering the right thing. Because the boss isn't telling you. I can't tell you how many times I've gone back to my office after a meeting, and I'm thinking, 'Are we doing the right movie? Are we doing the movie the right way? Am I delivering?'

"This isn't a science. It's a creative business."

As Anna makes so clear, this kind of "management curiosity" ripples into the corners of how people think about their work, and their approach to their work, every day.

Questions create both the authority in people to come up with ideas and take action, and the responsibility for moving things forward.

Questions create the space for all kinds of ideas, and the sparks to come up with those ideas.

Most important, questions send a very clear message: we're willing to listen, even to ideas or suggestions or problems we weren't expecting.

As valuable as questions are when you're the boss, I think they are just as important in every other direction in the workplace. People should ask their bosses questions. I appreciate it when people ask me the same kind of open-ended questions I so often ask.

What are you hoping for?

What are you expecting?

What's the most important part of this for you?

Those kinds of questions allow a boss to be clear about things that the boss might *think* are clear, but which often aren't clear at all.

Indeed, people at all levels should ask each other questions. That helps break down the barriers between job functions in our company, and in any workplace, and also helps puncture the idea that the job hierarchy determines who can have a good idea.

I like when people at Imagine ask me questions for many reasons, but here's the simplest and most powerful reason: if they ask the question, then they almost always listen to the answer.

People are more likely to consider a piece of advice, or a flat-out instruction, if they've asked for it in the first place.

Imagine is hardly a perfect workplace. We have our share of dull meetings and unproductive brainstorming sessions. We miscommunicate, we misinterpret, we miss out on some opportunities, and we push forward some projects we should let go.

But nobody is afraid to ask a question.

Nobody is afraid to answer a question.

Making questions a central part of managing people and projects is hard. I do it instinctively, from years of using questions to draw people out, and from a natural inclination to hear how projects are moving along rather than giving orders about them.

I think questions are an underappreciated management tool. But if it's not the way you normally interact with people, it will take a conscious effort to change. And you have to be prepared that, initially, asking questions slows things down. If you really want to know what people think, if you really want people to take more responsibility, if you really want a conversation around the problems and opportunities—rather than having people execute marching orders—that takes more time.

It's like being a reporter inside your own organization.

If asking questions isn't your typical style, this approach may puzzle people at first. So the best way to start might be to pick a particular project, and manage that project with questions. If you can start using curiosity in the office, you'll find that after a while, the benefits are remarkable. People's creativity gradually blossoms. And you end up knowing a lot more—you know more about the people you work with every day, and how their minds work, and you know more about what's going on with the work itself.

The most important element of this kind of culture is that you can't simply unleash a welter of questions—like a police detective or a lawyer doing a cross-examination in court. We're not asking questions for the sake of hearing ourselves ask them.

There are two key elements to a questioning culture. The first is the atmosphere around the question. You can't ask a question in a tone of voice or with a facial expression that indicates you already know the answer. You can't ask a question with that impatience that indicates you can't wait to ask the next question.

The point of the question has to be the answer.

The questions and the answers have to be driving a project or a decision forward.

And you have to listen to the answer. You have to take the answer seriously—as a boss or a colleague or a subordinate. If you don't take the answers seriously, no one will take the questions seriously. You'll just get the answers calculated to get everyone out of the conversation quickly.

The questions, in other words, have to come from genuine curiosity. If you're not curious enough to listen to the answer, all the question does is increase cynicism and decrease trust and engagement.

. . .

ONE OF MY CHILDHOOD heroes was Jonas Salk, the physician and scientist who figured out how to create the first vaccine that prevented polio. Salk was a towering figure.

Today, it's hard to imagine how much fear polio instilled in American parents and children. A devastating disease, polio is a viral infection of the lining of the spinal cord, and it killed children, left them permanently crippled, or left them paralyzed so severely that they had to live their lives inside an iron breathing machine called an iron lung. Polio is incurable and untreatable. Kids with a stiff or painful neck would be raced to the doctor or the hospital, and in some cases they would be dead within a few hours.

And polio is contagious, although how exactly it spread wasn't clear during the height of the epidemics. So when epidemics swept through the United States, people would keep their kids home from any place where crowds gathered—kids didn't go to the movies, summer camp, the beach, or the swimming pool.

In 1952, the year after I was born, there was a major epidemic of polio in the United States—58,000 people got the disease, 3,145 died, 21,269 were left with some level of paralysis.[3]

Just in the entertainment world, the number of people who survived polio gives a vivid sense of how widespread and dangerous it was. Alan Alda had polio as a child, as did Mia Far-row, Mel Ferrer, Francis Ford Coppola, Donald Sutherland, Johnny Weissmuller. Arthur C. Clarke, the science fiction author, had polio, as did the great newspaper editor Ben Bradlee, and the violinist Itzhak Perlman, who still requires braces and a crutch to walk.[4]

Jonas Salk was a determined and fairly independent-minded virologist who developed a "killed-virus" form of the polio vaccine while working at the University of Pittsburgh. The vaccine used inactivated particles of polio virus to stimulate the immune system, so people who received two doses of the vaccine were immune to infection.[5]

When the Salk vaccine was announced in 1955, Salk became a nationwide, and then a worldwide, hero. Immunization programs were launched immediately, and by the end of the 1950s, there were only a few hundred cases of polio being reported in the whole country. Tens of thousands of people were saved from lives of challenge, or from death. Everyone was able to go back to living without the shadow of polio over their lives.[6]

Dr. Salk was born in 1914, and he was just forty when the vaccine was announced. By the time I decided to meet him, he had established a scientific research center called the Salk Institute for Biological Research in La Jolla, California, just north of San Diego.

Salk was then in his late sixties and hard to reach, almost impossible.

I worked for more than a year just to get the attention of

someone in his office. Eventually, I discovered that Dr. Salk's assistant was a woman named Joan Abrahamson, who was herself a MacArthur Award winner, a so-called "genius grant" winner.

I talked to her regularly. She knew how much I admired Dr. Salk, and also how interested I was in meeting him. And she knew that Dr. Salk, while he kept a low profile, was not a classic absentminded scientist. Dr. Salk had a wide range of interests, and might enjoy learning something about the movie business.

It was 1984, not long after *Splash* had been released, when Joan told me that Dr. Salk would be speaking at a scientific meeting at the Beverly Wilshire Hotel, in Beverly Hills, and that if I wanted to meet them there in the morning, he could spend some time with me between sessions.

Not perfect, of course. Huge association meetings tend to be crowded, distracting, and filled with hubbub. But I certainly wasn't saying no. The morning of the meeting, I woke up feeling a little fluey. I was tired, light-headed, my throat a little tickly.

By the time I got to the Beverly Wilshire that morning, I think I looked a little sick. If it had been anything but meeting Jonas Salk, I would have wheeled around and headed back home.

I met Joan, and I met Dr. Salk. It was late morning. Dr. Salk looked at me with a little concern and he said, "What's wrong?"

I said, "Dr. Salk, I'm just not feeling that well this morning. I feel a little light-headed, a little sick."

He immediately said, "Let me go grab you a glass of orange juice." And before I could say anything, he popped off to the restaurant and came back with a big glass of orange juice.

This was long before most people had heard about the research that orange juice could really help perk you up if you were just getting sick. He said, "Drink this, it will bump up your blood sugar, you'll feel better quickly."

I drank the entire glass, and he was right, it worked.

It was kind of a surprising first encounter. Dr. Salk was so accessible, so human, so perceptive—he wasn't some genius off in his own world. He behaved, in fact, like a physician. He noticed immediately that something wasn't right, and he wanted to take care of me.

That morning, our conversation was brief, no more than thirty minutes. Dr. Salk was a slight-framed man, very friendly, very engaged, very intellectual. We talked a little about his research at the Salk Institute (he spent a lot of time trying to find a vaccine for HIV near the end of his career), and we talked about the impact of saving so many people's lives. He was completely modest about that.

Dr. Salk ended up inviting me to visit the Salk Institute, which I did, and we developed a friendship. He was intrigued with the idea of my curiosity conversations, and he proposed an expanded version. He suggested that the two of us each invite a couple of really interesting people to a daylong conversation, to be held at my Malibu house. So there would be six or eight of us, from totally different disciplines, spending the day in a relaxed atmosphere, trading our problems and our experiences and our questions. What a fabulous idea. And we did it.

Dr. Salk invited a robotics expert from Caltech and Betty Edwards, the theorist and teacher who wrote the book *Drawing on the Right Side of the Brain*. I brought director and producer Sydney Pollack (*Out of Africa, Tootsie*) and producer George Lucas, the creator of *Star Wars* and *Indiana Jones*, and George brought Linda Ronstadt, the singer who was his girlfriend at the time.

The whole thing was Dr. Salk's idea. He was curious—in particular, he was curious about how the "media mind" worked, how people like Lucas and Pollack thought about the world and what they created, and he was curious about storytelling. It was very relaxed, very unpretentious. We didn't solve the problems of the world, but we sure did put in one room a half dozen people who wouldn't typically encounter each other.

The time I remember most vividly with Jonas Salk, though, was the first moment we met—that honest, simple, human connection right at the beginning. Although he was just in the process of meeting me, Dr. Salk noticed I was looking down and was considerate enough to ask why—and immediately offered help. These days, it seems, it's almost a shock when people ask questions about you, and then stop long enough to absorb the answer.

Curiosity is what creates empathy. To care about someone, you have to wonder about them.

Curiosity creates interest. It can also create excitement.

A good first date is filled with a tumble of questions and answers, the fizz of discovering someone new, of learning how they connect to you, and of how they are different. You can't decide whether it's more fun to ask questions of your date, or to answer your date's questions about you.

But what happens months or years later is that your boy-friend or girlfriend, your husband or wife, feels familiar. That's the beauty and safety of a solid, intimate relationship: you feel like you know the person, like you can rely on the person and their responses, that you can, perhaps, even predict them.

You love that person. You love the version of that person that you hold in your mind and your heart.

But familiarity is the enemy of curiosity.

And when our curiosity about those closest to us fades, that's the moment when our connection begins to fray. It frays silently, almost invisibly. But when we stop asking genuine questions of those around us—and most important, when we stop really listening to the answers—that's when we start to lose our connection.

What happened at the office today, dear?

Not much. How about you?

If you picture for a moment the image of a married couple, in their mid-thirties, they've got the two kids put to sleep, it's nine o'clock at night, they're tired, they're cleaning up the kitchen or they're folding laundry or they're sitting in the family room, or they're getting ready for bed. They're thinking about all the ordinary things that crowd into your brain when the day quiets down: Did I remember to RSVP for that birthday party? How am I going to deal with Sally at that project review tomorrow? I wonder why Tom has been so chilly recently? I forgot to make those plane reservations again! The conversation between the couple is desultory, or it's purely pragmatic—you do this, I'll do that.

Maybe it's just a moment of tiredness and quiet before bed. But if you string a month of evenings like that together, if you string a year of evenings like that together, that's how people drift apart.

The familiarity is comfortable, even reassuring. But the couple has stopped being curious about each other—genuinely curious. They don't ask real questions. They don't listen to the answers.

It's a little simplistic, of course, but the quickest way to restore energy and excitement to your relationships is to bring some real curiosity back to them. Ask questions about your spouse's day, and pay attention to the answers. Ask questions about your kids' friends, about their classes, about what's exciting them at school, and pay attention to the answers.

Ask questions like you would have on a first date—ask about their feelings, their reactions.

How do you feel about . . . ?

What did you think of . . . ?

What doesn't work are the classic questions we all ask too often: What happened at work? What happened at school?

Those questions can be waved off. "Nothing." That's the answer 95 percent of the time. As if your wife spent eight hours at the office or your kids spent eight hours at school staring silently at a blank wall—and then came home.

You need questions that can't be answered with a single muttered word.

What did Sally think of your new ideas for the product launch?

Are you enjoying Mr. Meyer's history class?

How are you thinking about your speech at the convention next week?

Who's going to try out for the musical this year?

Maybe we should have an adventure this weekend. What would you like to do Saturday afternoon?

How many marriages that drift into disconnection and boredom could be helped by a revival of genuine curiosity on both sides? We need these daily reminders that although I live with this person, I don't actually know her *today*—unless I ask about her today.

We don't just take our relationships to those closest to us for granted. We take for granted that we know them so well, we know what happened today. We know what they think.

But we don't. That's part of the fun of curiosity, and part of the value of curiosity: it creates the moment of surprise.

And before the moment of surprise comes the moment of respect. Genuine curiosity requires respect—I care about you, and I care about your experience in the world, and I want to hear about it.

This brings me back to Ron Howard. I feel like I know Ron

as well as I know anyone, and I certainly rely on him in professional and personal terms. But I never presume I know what's happening with Ron, and I never presume that I know what his reaction to something is going to be. I ask.

That same kind of respect, curiosity, and surprise is just as powerful in our intimate relationships as it is at work. In that sense, every conversation can be a curiosity conversation. It's another example of curiosity being fundamentally respectful—you aren't just asking about the person you're talking to, you are genuinely interested in what she has to say, in her point of view, in her experiences.

At work, you can manage people by talking at them—but you can't manage them very well by doing that. To be a good manager, you need to understand the people you work with, and if you're doing all the talking, you can't understand them.

And if you don't understand the people you're working with, you certainly can't inspire them.

At home, you can be in the same room as your partner or your kids, but you can't be connected to them unless you can ask questions about them and hear the answers. Curiosity is the door to open those relationships, and to reopen them. It can keep you from being lonely.

And by the way: I love people being curious about me. I like it when people ask me interesting questions, I like a great conversation, and I like telling stories. It's almost as much fun to be the object of curiosity as it is to be curious.

Curiosity isn't necessarily about achieving something—about driving toward some goal.

Sometimes, it's just about connecting with people. Which is to say, curiosity can be about sustaining intimacy. It's not about a goal, it's about happiness.

. . .

YOUR LOVE FOR SOMEONE can, of course, also fire your curiosity on their behalf.

My oldest son, Riley, was born in 1986. When he was about three and a half years old, we realized there was something different about his nervous system, about his psychology, and his responses. Riley's mom, Corki—then my wife—and I spent many years trying to understand what was happening with him developmentally, and when he was about seven years old, he was diagnosed with Asperger's syndrome.

It was the early nineties, and treatment for Asperger's then was even more uncertain than it is today. Riley was a happy kid. He was socially oriented. We wanted to help him connect with the world in the most constructive way possible.

We tried different styles of education. We tried some weird glasses that changed his vision. We tried Ritalin—though only briefly. Getting Riley the help he needs has been a constant journey, for him and for his mother and for me.

As Riley was growing up, I started thinking about mental illness, and the stigma attached to it. I had survived stigma myself, of course, because of my reading disability. Riley is a gracious and delightful person, but if you don't understand how the world looks to him, you might be puzzled by him. I wanted to do a movie that really tackled the issues around mental illness, that helped destigmatize it. I was always watching for an idea.

In the spring of 1998, Graydon Carter, the editor of *Vanity Fair*, called and told me I had to read a piece in the June issue, an excerpt from a book by Sylvia Nasar called *A Beautiful Mind*, that told the life story of John Nash, a Princeton-educated mathematician who won the Nobel Prize, but who was also plagued with devastating schizophrenia. The magazine excerpt was riveting. Here was a story about genius and schizophrenia braided together—of achievement, mental illness, and overcoming stigma—all in the life of a real man. I was thinking about Riley even as I was reading the pages in *Vanity Fair*.

I immediately knew two things. I wanted to make a movie of *A Beautiful Mind* and the life of the Nobel laureate mathematician who was also schizophrenic. And I wanted it to be the kind of movie that would reach people and change their attitudes, even change their behavior, toward people who are different—disabled or mentally ill.

Part of the power of *A Beautiful Mind* comes from this remarkable insight: It isn't just hard for outsiders to relate to someone who is different. It's hard for the person who is mentally ill to relate to everyone else. That person struggles to understand how the world works too, and struggles to understand people's responses to him.

There was an auction for the movie rights to *A Beautiful*

Mind, and as part of the auction, I sat and talked to Sylvia Nasar, and also to John Nash himself, and his wife, Alicia. They wanted to know why I wanted to make the movie, and what kind of movie I wanted to make.

I talked a little bit about my son, but mostly I talked about John Nash's story. I'd already produced two movies at that point that involved buying the rights to the stories of real people—*The Doors* and *Apollo 13.* You have to tell people the truth about the movie you want to make from their lives—you have to tell them the truth, and if you get the movie, you have to stick to what you promised.

I told John Nash that I wouldn't portray him as a perfect person. He's brilliant, but also arrogant, a tough guy. That's important. He has a beautiful love story with his wife. I said, "I want to do a movie that celebrates the beauty of your mind and your romance."

And that's the movie we made—that's the movie the screenwriter, Akiva Goldsman, was able to write, the movie Ron Howard created on screen as director, those are the people that Russell Crowe and Jennifer Connelly were able to bring to life so vividly.

While we were in the early stages of working on the movie, I was thinking about how to convey how the mind of a schizophrenic works—how to show that on screen. Sylvia Nasar's book doesn't have this sense of alternate reality. But I didn't want the movie of *A Beautiful Mind* to simply portray John Nash from the point of view of the people around him. That wouldn't provide the revelation or the connection we were looking for.

The solution came one day before *A Beautiful Mind* was too far along. Riley and I were watching Stanley Kubrick's *The Shining* together. There's a vivid scene in *The Shining* where Jack Nicholson is in a bar, having conversations with people who don't exist. It hit me immediately. I thought we should find a way of showing Nash's reality—show how the schizophrenic mind works by showing what the world looks like from his point of view. And that's what we did: John Nash's reality is shown in the movie no differently than everyone else's reality.

Akiva Goldsman got that idea perfectly—and I think it's the source of the power of the movie itself, in addition to the portrayals by Russell and Jennifer, of course.

The movie was more than a success. It did well financially. It won four Academy Awards—for Ron and me for best picture, for Ron for best director, for Akiva for best adapted screenplay, for Jennifer for best supporting actress. And John and Alicia Nash were with us at the Academy Awards that night in 2002.

But the real success is that the movie has affected so many people's lives. People came up to me on the street—people still come up to me—and say, You've helped me understand what my child or my niece or my mother is going through. I remember being at a Ralph's supermarket in Malibu not long after the movie came out, and a woman came up to me and told me she was brought to tears by that movie.

It isn't just that I did *A Beautiful Mind* because the story touched me personally. The way we did it came directly from my own experiences. And the way we did it, to me, makes it such a powerful, and such a valuable, movie. My curiosity and determination to help Riley led me to *A Beautiful Mind*. And my experience being his father, and watching how he experiences the world, led us to a totally original treatment of mental illness. *A Beautiful Mind* is unquestionably the most gratifying movie I've ever made.

CHAPTER SIX

Good Taste and the Power of Anti-Curiosity

"If we are not able to ask skeptical questions, to interrogate those who tell us that something is true, to be skeptical of those in authority, then we are up for grabs for the next charlatan—political or religious—who comes ambling along."

—*Carl Sagan*[1]

THE MOVIES WE'VE MADE AT Imagine have a great variety of settings, stories, and tones.

We made a movie about achieving the American dream— and the central character was a semiliterate African American man trying to climb the ladder of the heroin trade in New York City in the 1970s. That movie, *American Gangster*, is also about the values of American capitalism.

We made a movie about the power and the passion of high school football in rural Texas. It's a movie about how boys grow up, how they discover who they really are; it's about teamwork and community and identity. It's also about disappointment, because at the climax of *Friday Night Lights*, the Permian High Panthers lose their big game.

We made a movie called *8 Mile* about a hip-hop artist—a white hip-hop artist.

We made a movie about the movie *Deep Throat*, and how that pornographic film about oral sex came to define a critical moment in our culture.

We made a movie about a Nobel Prize–winning mathematician—but *A Beautiful Mind* is really about what it's like to be mentally ill, to be schizophrenic, and to try to function in the world anyway.

Two things are true about all these movies.

First, they are all about developing character, about discovering flaws and strengths, and overcoming your emotional injuries to become a full person. To me, the American dream is about overcoming obstacles—the circumstances of your birth, a limited education, the way other people perceive you, something inside your own head. Overcoming obstacles is itself an art form. So if the movies I make have a single theme, it is how to leverage your limits into success.

Second, no one in Hollywood really wanted to do any of them.

I've talked about using curiosity to get around the "no" that is so common in Hollywood and at work in general. The first reaction to most ideas that are a little outside the mainstream is discomfort, and the first reaction to discomfort is to say "no."

Why are we glorifying a heroin dealer?[2]

Shouldn't the football team win the big game?

Who wants to watch a whole movie about a struggling white hip-hop artist?

For me, curiosity helps find ideas that are edgy and different and interesting. Curiosity provides the wide range of experience and understanding of popular culture that gives me an instinct of when something new might resonate. And curiosity gives me courage, the courage to have confidence in those interesting ideas, even if they aren't popular ideas.

Sometimes you don't just want to attract the crowd to something mainstream, you want to create the crowd for something unconventional.

I like projects with soul—stories and characters with heart. I like to believe in something. I like the idea of the popular iconoclast—doing work that is at the edge, but not too far over the edge.

That's when I run into something very important, and very contrarian. I run into the limits of curiosity.

Sometimes you need anti-curiosity.

When I have an idea I love that is unconventional, eventually I have to say, "I'm doing it."

Don't tell me why it's a bad idea—I'm doing it. That's anti-curiosity.

Anti-curiosity isn't just the determination to grab hold of an interesting idea and push forward in the face of skepticism and rejection. Anti-curiosity is something much more specific and important.

It's the moment when you shut down your curiosity, when you resist learning more, when you may have to tell people, No, that's okay, don't tell me all your reasons for saying no.

Here's what I mean. When you're building financial and casting support for a movie, you have already built the case for the movie for yourself, in your own mind. You have gone over and over why this story is interesting, why the script is good, why the people you want to make the movie match the story and the script.

Everyone in Hollywood knows how to "make the case." That's what we do with each other all day long. And any successful producer or director or actor is great at "making the case."

When someone tells me "no," you'd think I'd be immediately curious about why they're saying "no." Maybe they're hung up on something small, something I could fix easily. Maybe four people in a row will make the same criticism, will give me the same reason they are saying "no"—and why wouldn't I want to know that? Maybe after I hear why an idea isn't winning support, like a smart politician reading the opinion polls, I'll change my mind.

But that doesn't work. You just end up reshaping an interesting, unconventional story into a different story to match the popular conception.

So when someone tells me "no," almost always, that's it. I don't want them to unfurl this long, persuasive argument about why they think my idea isn't any good, or isn't right for them, or could be much better if I reconfigured it somehow.

I decline all that input because I'm worried about being persuaded out of something I really believe in. I'm worried about being persuaded into something I don't believe in—just because someone smart and persuasive is sitting in front of me, making *their* case.

If I've formed an opinion on something fundamental like a movie we should do, if I've dedicated a lot of time to it, a lot of money, a lot of curiosity, then I don't want any more information on it. I don't want you trying to "recontextualize" an artistic decision that I've made.

Thanks anyway, I don't want your critique.

Because here's another thing I know for sure.

You don't know what a good idea is.

At least, you don't know what a good idea is any more than I know what a good idea is. No one in Hollywood really knows what a good idea is before a movie hits the screens. We only know if it's a *good* idea after it's done.

That's not about success, by the way. At Imagine, we've done some movies that were successful, but weren't necessarily great movies. Much more important, we've done some great movies that weren't huge box office hits—*Rush*, *Get On Up*, *Frost/Nixon*, *The Doors*.

In advance, my passion for something I think is a good idea, an interesting idea, is just as valid as someone's decision that it isn't. But the certainty that something is a worthwhile idea is fragile. It requires energy and determination and optimism to keep going. I don't want other people's negativity to get inside my head, to undermine my confidence. I don't need to hear a list of criticisms—whether it's sincere or not. When you're trying to get a movie made, when you're making your case, you've spent months or years working on something, and you need to develop a kind of invulnerability if you're both going to get it made, and protect it.

When I'm checking in with people I want to join us, it works something like this.

I'll send out the script, I'll send out all the information—I'm the producer, Ron Howard is the director, here's the budget, here's the cast.

After a little while, I get on the phone. They'll say, "We're going to pass."

I'll say, "You're passing? Honestly? Are you *sure* you're passing? Okay, then, thank you very much. I really appreciate you reading it."

If it's something I think is really right for the person I'm talking to—if I think they're the ones making a mistake—I might say, "You can't say no! You gotta say yes!"

But that's it. No curiosity. The wall goes up. Anti-curiosity.

Because I don't need someone casting doubt, when they've spent an hour thinking about the project, and I've spent three years thinking about it. If they're saying no, I need all my determination and confidence to grab hold of the idea and take it to the next person with the same level of passion and enthusiasm. You can't get anything done trying to absorb and neutralize everyone else's criticisms.

There have been moments when I've been a little too quick with my anti-curiosity. Ron Howard and I took Imagine Entertainment public in 1986.[3] We thought it would be an innovative way to run a creative company. But public companies are much more complicated to run than private companies—and that turns out to be particularly true in a hit-and-miss kind of business like movie and TV production. We were undercapitalized. We were uncomfortable with all the rules about public companies—what we had to reveal, what we could talk about, what we couldn't talk about. After seven years, in 1993, Ron and I bought the company back from the shareholders. Before we went public, we certainly hadn't been nearly curious enough about what being a "public" company would require of us.

When it comes to movies, there is one really memorable case where I shouldn't have suspended my curiosity—the quirky movie *Cry-Baby* from 1990. Curiosity got me into that movie. A script came in from director John Waters. I read it. I was attracted to it.

I had just seen *Hairspray*, which Waters had written and directed, and I loved it. I thought *Cry-Baby* could either be a flop, or an unexpected hit like *Grease*. I said yes. We got an incredible cast to work with John Waters—Johnny Depp as the lead (it was his big movie break), and also Willem Dafoe, Patty Hearst, Troy Donahue, Joey Heatherton, Iggy Pop, Traci Lords.

I loved working with John Waters. I loved working with Johnny Depp. But here's what I didn't do: I didn't go back and see John Waters's other movies. A couple of people told me to—before you pay for a John Waters movie, they said, go watch a bunch of John Waters movies. He's not exactly mainstream. They said, at least watch *Pink Flamingos*, which is pretty edgy, before you green-light *Cry-Baby*.

I was having none of it. I didn't want any of that hesitation in my psyche. I'd decided I was being curious enough—curious enough to see what happened with this John Waters film.

At the box office, *Cry-Baby* was a flop.

The lesson is pretty clear: I should have watched John Waters's previous movies. I should have watched *Pink Flamingos*. I didn't live with that script at all. I got excited, and I didn't want to second-guess my instincts.

So how do you know when not to be curious?

It looks harder to figure out than it really is.

Most of the time, curiosity is energizing. It motivates you.

It takes you to places you haven't been before, it introduces you to people you haven't met before, it teaches you something new about people you know already.

Sometimes curiosity carries you to places that are hugely unpleasant or painful, but important. It's hard to read about child abuse, it's hard to read about war, it's hard to hear about the painful experiences of people you love. But in all those kinds of cases, you have an obligation to learn, to listen, to understand.

Sometimes you have to listen to people offering criticism of yourself—a smart boss might have great advice about how to be more effective at work, about how to write better, or how to be more persuasive. A colleague might be able to tell you how you sabotage yourself, or undermine your work, or damage relationships you need to be nurturing.

In those instances, there's something constructive coming from the curiosity, from listening, even though the conversation itself might be unpleasant.

You know to stop being curious when your results are just the opposite of what you need—when they sap your momentum, drain your enthusiasm, corrode your confidence. When you're getting a critique but not much in the way of useful ideas, that's the moment for a pinch of anti-curiosity.

. . .

I ADMIT THAT I don't know specifically where interesting ideas come from. But I know generally: they come from mixing a lot of experiences, information, and perspectives, then noticing something unusual or revealing or new. But it's not that important to know where good ideas come from. It's important to recognize what you think is an interesting idea when you see it.

That presents a problem, of course, because I just said that no one in Hollywood really knows what a good idea is until we see it out there in the world.

But I do know what I think is a good idea, an interesting idea, when I see it.

A TV series built around catching a terrorist, where the good guy is racing the clock in real time. That's an interesting idea.

A movie about how one man—one very smart and also very strange man—came to shape the FBI for forty years, and thus shape crime fighting and America itself. That's an interesting idea.

Jim Carrey as a lawyer who can't tell a lie for twenty-four hours. That's an interesting idea.

Tom Hanks as a Harvard professor who needs to find the Holy Grail in order to clear himself of murder charges, and in the process uncovers the deepest secrets of the Catholic Church. That's an interesting idea.

All these ideas worked out really well—I thought they were good ideas, we brought together a team behind each one of them, and that team made good movies and TV shows.

We've had interesting ideas that didn't work out that well. How about Russell Crowe as a washed-up 1920s boxer who makes a tremendous comeback, and becomes world champion? That was the movie *Cinderella Man*, which wasn't a big hit with moviegoers. But it's a good movie.

How about a movie dramatizing David Frost's four interviews with disgraced president Richard Nixon? It also wasn't a big hit with moviegoers. But *Frost/Nixon* is a good movie—it received five Oscar nominations and five Golden Globe nominations.

You may or may not like those TV shows or movies. The important thing is that I thought they were worthwhile ideas when they came to me, I recognized them as interesting. I worked passionately to develop each of them. I didn't just think they were interesting ideas, I believed they were, and then I acted like they were interesting ideas.

So how did I know they were worthwhile?

It's a question of taste.

They were good ideas—in my opinion. But my opinion about something like a movie or a TV show isn't the same as the opinion of a person buying a ticket and a bucket of popcorn to see *Liar Liar* or *Cinderella Man*.

My "opinion" about this kind of storytelling is based on decades of experience—listening to people talk about movie ideas, reading their pitches, reading their scripts, seeing what happens between idea and script and screen. My opinion is based on understanding, over and over, the work necessary to create movies and TV shows of quality—and trying to understand why quality sometimes matters to popularity, and why it sometimes doesn't.

My opinion is based on something people outside show business never see—all the things I say "no" to. Because I say "no" as much as anyone. The stories that we get pitched and don't make are as important a measure of taste as the ones we do. We are trying to make movies we love, as I tried to make clear in the conversation I had about the stalled movie. We're trying to make movies with a sense of good taste about them.

I do think I have good taste in movies. But it is clearly my own sense of taste about them. Steven Spielberg has good taste about movies, James Cameron has good taste about movies— but their movies look nothing like our movies.

If you have good taste, three things are true. First, you have the ability to judge the quality of something, whether it's music or art, architecture or cooking, movies or books. Second, your sense of whether something is worthwhile is individual—you bring a perspective to your judgments. And third, there is also something universal about your judgments—your taste can be understood and appreciated by people who aren't as experienced as you, whose sense of taste isn't as well developed as yours. Your good taste is educated, it has a splash of individuality about it, and also a certain breadth of appeal.

That's what taste is, in fact: an educated, experienced opinion that you can articulate, and with which other people can agree or argue.

What I think is a good idea comes from applying my forty years of experience—my taste—to the ideas that come my way. It's a little more complicated than that, of course—I may think something is a good idea that isn't commercially viable; or I may pick the occasional project that's just fun, that doesn't really hit the top of the curve in terms of taste, but is very entertaining.

So to find interesting ideas, to have good ideas, most of us need curiosity.

And to recognize those ideas with real confidence you need good taste.

And to develop that sense of taste—of personal style and experienced judgment—you also need curiosity.

That's where my sense of taste comes from, in large part: curiosity—and experience.

If you've only ever heard one song, say, "Gimme Shelter" by the Rolling Stones, you can't have a well-developed sense of music taste. If your experience with art is only seeing Andy Warhol—or only seeing Andrew Wyeth—you can't have an evolved sense of taste about art.

You may say, hey, I really liked that song. Or hey, I really didn't care for those paintings by Andrew Wyeth. But that's not taste, that's opinion.

Developing a sense of taste means exposing yourself to a wide range of something—a wide range of music, a wide range of art—and not just exposing yourself, but asking questions. Why is Andy Warhol considered a great artist? What was he thinking when he did his art? What do other people think of his art—people with well-developed taste? What other art was being produced at the same time as Warhol's? What are his best pieces? Who thinks his art is great? What other artists did Warhol influence? What other parts of the culture did Warhol influence?

Obviously, it helps to like what you're paying attention to, because developing a sense of taste requires commitment. There's no point in developing a sense of taste about hip-hop music if you really don't like listening to hip-hop music; the same is true of opera.

The point of all that curiosity isn't to persuade you to have the same opinion as anyone else about Andy Warhol. It's to give you a framework for understanding his work. You still have your own reaction—you can say, I understand the importance of Andy Warhol, but I don't really like his art. It's not to my taste.

And the point of all that curiosity isn't to turn something fun—like music—into a chore. We all know people who are totally immersed in contemporary music. They know every new band, they know every new style, they know who produces who, they know who influences who. Music aficionados like that make great playlists. They do it precisely because they love music. Their curiosity flows so naturally that it's a passion.

Taste is opinion, framed by the context of what you're judging. And taste gives you confidence in your judgment. Taste gives you confidence that you understand more than what you simply like—you understand what's good and what's not. It's taste that helps give you the judgment to assess something new. To be able to ask, and answer, the question, "Is that a good idea?"

For me, the dozens of curiosity conversations I've had are the foundation for developing a sense of taste about music, art, architecture, about popular culture in general. They give me an informed filter for assessing what comes my way—whether it's movie ideas, or a conversation about developments in particle physics, or electronic dance music. I don't think it gives me a "better" filter—my taste is my own. But it definitely gives me a more informed filter. I'm always talking to people with deep experience—and deeply educated taste themselves—about the things I care about. That curiosity gives me confidence in my own judgments.

There's one small caveat to using curiosity to develop good taste. Not everyone gets a sense of taste about art or music or food driven by their own curiosity and energy. If you grow up with parents who care about opera, who fill the house with classical music or modern art, poetry, or fine cuisine, you may well arrive at adulthood with a very well-developed sense of taste about those things. Especially as a child, you can develop taste based on immersion. That may be the best way to develop a sense of taste, in fact, but it's not an opportunity most of us have. And it's certainly not an opportunity we get to choose.

. . .

CURIOSITY EQUIPS US WITH the skills for openhearted, open-minded exploration. That's the quality of my curiosity conversations.

Curiosity also gives us the skills to zero in on the answer to a question. That's the quality of a police detective driven to solve a murder. That's the quality of a physician determined to figure out what disease is causing a patient's set of oddly contradictory symptoms and test results.

And curiosity gives us the skills to better relate to people, and to better manage and work with them in professional settings. That's the quality of my asking questions in the office. I'm not quite having an open-ended conversation with Anna Culp or our other executives about the state of our movies in production, but I'm also not pursuing specific answers with the relentless zeal of a police detective. Those kinds of conversations are a kind of accountability curiosity—open to hearing what's going on, but asking questions with a specific purpose in mind.

I think developing a sense of taste about something—or more broadly, a sense of judgment—falls into this third quality of curiosity. It's about being curious, but with a purpose or a goal in mind. I'm not asking about the progress on our movies because I'm idly interested in how things are going. I'm doing my part to move things along with the goal of getting those movies made, made well, made on budget, made on time. I'm doing it while deferring to my colleague's judgment and autonomy, but we both know that although I'm asking questions, I'm using them to hold her and the movie itself accountable.

Taste works the same way. You take your experience and your judgment and your preferences, and you apply them with openness but also some skepticism to whatever comes your way—ideas, songs, meals, an acting performance. You're using taste and a skeptical curiosity to ask: How good is this thing I'm being asked to consider? How enjoyable is it? Where does it fit into what I already know?

Your good taste can discover things that are thrilling. It can save you from mediocrity. But it is skeptical. Using your judgment always involves raising your eyebrow, it means starting with a question mark: how good is this thing—how interesting, how original, how high-quality—given everything else I know?

There is one more quality of curiosity that we haven't touched on yet, and that's the quality of curiosity that the astronomer and author Carl Sagan refers to in the opening quote of this chapter: the value of curiosity in managing our public life, our democracy.

Democracy requires accountability. In fact, accountability is the very point of democracy—to understand what needs to be done in the community, to discuss it, to weigh the options, to make decisions, and then to assess whether those decisions were right and hold the people who made the decisions accountable for them.

That's why we have a free press—to ask questions. That's why we have elections—to ask whether we want to retain the people who hold public office. That's why the proceedings of the House and Senate and the courts are open to all, as are the meetings of every city council, county commission, and school board in the nation. It's why we have three branches of government in the United States, in fact—to create a system of accountability among Congress, the presidency, and the courts.

In a society as complicated as ours, we often outsource that accountability. We let the press ask the questions (and then criticize the press for not asking the right questions). We let Congress ask the questions (and then criticize Congress for being either too timid or too destructive). We let activists ask the questions (and then criticize them for being too partisan).

Ultimately, the accountability has to come from the citizens. We need to be curious about how our government is functioning—whether it's the local high school or the VA health-care system, NASA's International Space Station or the finances of Social Security. What is the government supposed to be doing? Is it doing that? If not, why not? Who, in particular, is responsible—and do we have a way of getting them to do what we want, or should we fire them?

The way American government is designed assumes our curiosity. It doesn't have the skepticism itself built in—that has to come from us—but it has the *opportunity* for the skepticism built in.

Curiosity is as powerful in the public sphere as it is, for instance, at work. The very act of showing up and asking questions at a local government hearing is a vivid reminder that the government is accountable to us, and not the other way around. The questions communicate both authority and a sense of our values—whether we're standing at the lectern at the school board meeting, or raising a hand at a candidate forum, or watching the House of Representatives on C-SPAN.

The connection between the personal curiosity we've been discussing and this more public curiosity is very simple: it's the habit of asking questions, of constantly reminding ourselves of the value of asking questions, and of our right to ask questions.

In fact, it's not just that democracy permits curiosity. Without curiosity, it's not democracy.

And the opposite is also true. Democracy happens to be the societal framework that gives freest rein to our curiosity in every other arena.

CHAPTER SEVEN

The Golden Age of Curiosity

"Perhaps one day men will no longer be interested in the unknown, no longer tantalized by mystery. This is possible, but when Man loses his curiosity one feels he will have lost most of the other things that make him human."

—*Arthur C. Clarke*[1]

WE WERE DRIVING IN THE car one afternoon with the windows open. It was 1959—I was eight years old. We stopped at a traffic light, and suddenly there was a bee buzzing around, in and out of the windows. It was making me nervous. I didn't want to get stung by the bee.

I couldn't wait for the light to change, for the car to get moving again. But all of a sudden I had a question: which moves faster—a car or a bee? Maybe the bee would be able to keep up with us, even after my mom pulled away from the intersection.

We eluded the bee that afternoon, but the question stuck with me. Which moves faster, a bee or a car? I tried to puzzle it out, but I didn't come to a satisfying answer. As an eight-year-old in 1959, I could do nothing with that question but ask a grown-up. So I did what I often did with my questions: I asked my grandmother. My grandmother was kind of my own personal Google—not quite as omniscient as the Internet seems to be, but much more understanding and encouraging.

She liked my questions even when she didn't know the answers.[2]

I've been curious for as long as I have memories of myself. I was thinking of myself as curious before I was thinking of myself as anything else. It is my first personality trait. Fifty years later, I think of myself as curious the way some people think of themselves as funny, or smart, or gregarious.

For me, being curious defines not just my personality, not just the way I think of myself, it has been the key to my survival and my success. It's how I survived my reading problems. It's how I survived a bumpy academic career. It's how I ended up in the movie business; it's how I figured out the movie business. And curiosity is the quality I think helps distinguish me in Hollywood.

I ask questions.

The questions spark interesting ideas. The questions build collaborative relationships. The questions create all kinds of connections—connections among unlikely topics, among unlikely collaborators. And the interesting ideas, the collaborative relationships, and the web of connections work together to build trust.

Curiosity isn't just a quality of my personality—it's at the heart of how I approach being alive. I think it has been the differentiator. I think it's one of the reasons people like to work with me, in a business where there are lots of producers to choose from.

Curiosity gave me the dream. It, quite literally, helped me create the life I imagined back when I was twenty-three years old. In fact, it's helped me create a life much more adventurous, interesting, and successful than I could have hoped for at age twenty-three.

For me, writing this book has meant thinking about curiosity in ways I never have, and it has revealed all kinds of qualities of curiosity itself that had never occurred to me before. In fact, I've tried to make curiosity itself a character in the book, because curiosity is available to anyone. My stories are meant to inspire you and entertain you—they are my experience of curiosity. But everyone gets to use curiosity to chase the things that are most important to them.

That's the wonderful way that curiosity is different from intelligence or creativity or even from leadership. Some people are really smart. Some people are really creative. Some people have galvanic leadership qualities. But not everyone.

But you can be as curious as you want to be, and it doesn't matter when you start. And your curiosity can help you be smarter and more creative, it can help you be more effective and also help you be a better person.

.   .   .

ONE OF THE THINGS I love about curiosity is that it is an instinct with many dualities. Curiosity has a very yin-and-yang quality about it. It's worth paying attention to those dualities, because they help us see curiosity more clearly.

For instance, you can unleash your curiosity, or it can unleash you. That is, you can decide you need to be curious about something. But once you get going, your curiosity will pull you along.

The more you limit curiosity—the more you tease people with what's coming without telling them—the more you increase their curiosity. Who killed J.R.? Who won the Mega Millions lottery jackpot?

Likewise, you can be intensely curious about something relatively minor, and the moment you know the answer, your curiosity is satisfied. Once you know who won the lottery, the instinct to be curious about that deflates completely.

You can be curious about something very specific—like whether a bee or a car moves faster—curious about something to which you can get a definitive answer. That may or may not open up new questions for you (how do bees manage to fly at twenty mph?). But you can also be curious about things to which you may never know the answer—physicians, psychologists, physicists, cosmologists are all researching areas where we learn more and more, and yet may never have definitive answers. That kind of curiosity can carry you through your entire life.

Curiosity requires a certain amount of bravery—the courage to reveal you don't know something, the courage to ask a question of someone. But curiosity can also give you courage. It requires confidence—just a little bit—but it repays you by building up your confidence.

Nothing unleashes curiosity in an audience like good storytelling. Nothing inspires storytelling, in turn, like the results of curiosity.

Curiosity can easily become a habit—the more you use it, the more naturally it will come to you. But you can also use curiosity actively—you can always overrule your natural pacing of asking questions and say to yourself, This is something I need to dig into. This is something, or someone, I need to know more about.

Curiosity looks like it's a "deconstructive" process. That seems almost obvious—by asking questions about things, you're taking them apart, you're trying to understand how they work, whether it's the engine in your Toyota Prius or the personality of your boss. But, in fact, curiosity isn't deconstructive. It's synthetic. When curiosity really captures you, it fits the pieces of the world together. You may have to learn about the parts, but when you're done, you have a picture of something you never understood before.

Curiosity is a tool of engagement with other people. But it's also the path to independence—independence of thought. Curiosity helps create collaboration, but it also helps give you autonomy.

Curiosity is wonderfully refreshing. You cannot use it up. In fact, the more curious you are today—about something specific, or in general—the more likely you are to be curious in the future. With one exception: curiosity hasn't inspired much curiosity about itself. We're curious about all kinds of things, except the concept of curiosity.

And finally, we live at a moment in time that should be a "golden age of curiosity." As individuals, we have access to more information more quickly than anyone has ever had before. Some places are taking advantage of this in big ways—companies in Silicon Valley are a vivid and instructive example. The energy and creativity of entrepreneurs comes from asking questions—questions like "What's next?" and "Why can't we do it *this* way?"

And yet, curiosity remains wildly undervalued today. In the structured settings where we could be teaching people how to harness the power of curiosity—schools, universities, workplaces—it often isn't encouraged. At best, it gets lip service. In many of those settings, curiosity isn't even a topic.

But just as each of us can start using our own curiosity the moment we decide to, we can help create that golden age of curiosity in the wider culture. We can do it in some simple ways, by answering every question our own children ask, and by helping them find the answers when we don't know them. We can do it, within our own power, at work in a whole range of small but invaluable ways: by asking questions ourselves; by treating questions from our colleagues with respect and seriousness; by welcoming questions from our customers and clients; by seeing those questions as opportunities, not interruptions. The point isn't to start asking a bunch of questions, rat-a-tat, like a prosecutor. The point is to gradually shift the culture—of your family, of your workplace—so we're making it safe to be curious. That's how we unleash a blossoming of curiosity, and all the benefits that come with it.

•   •   •

ROBERT HOOKE WAS A brilliant seventeenth-century English scientist who helped usher in the era of scientific inquiry—moving society away from religious explanations of how the world worked toward a scientific understanding.

Hooke was a contemporary and fierce rival of Isaac Newton; some have compared Hooke's range of interests and skills to Leonardo da Vinci. Hooke contributed discoveries, advances, and lasting insights to physics, architecture, astronomy, paleontology, and biology. He lived from 1635 to 1703, but although he's been dead three hundred years, he contributed to the engineering of modern clocks, microscopes, and cars. It was

Hooke, peering through a microscope at a razor-thin slice of the bark of a cork tree, who first used the word "cell" to describe the basic unit of biology he saw in the viewfinder.[3]

This range of expertise is astonishing today, in an era when so many people, even scientists, are so specialized. The kinds of discoveries and insights made by someone like Hooke are thrilling. But what is really humbling is that scientists like Hooke didn't just revolutionize how we understand the world—from the motions of the planets to the biology of our own bodies. They had to *be* revolutionaries. They were fighting contempt, mockery, and two thousand years of power structure that not only set strict limits on how each member of society could operate, but also what it was okay to ask questions about.

As the scholar of curiosity Barbara Benedict explained when we talked to her, "One of the things that made the seventeenth- and eighteenth-century scientists really extraordinary is that they asked questions that hadn't been asked before."

Hooke, she pointed out, "looked at his own urine under the microscope. That was hugely transgressive. No one had ever thought to look at urine as a subject of scientific examination."

Benedict is a literary scholar—she's the Charles A. Dana professor of English Literature at Trinity College in Connecticut—and she became captivated by curiosity because she kept coming across the word, and the idea, while studying eighteenth-century literature. "I came across the word 'curious' so often in every text, I got a little irritated," Benedict said. "What does it mean when you call someone 'the curious reader'? Is that a compliment or not?"

Benedict was so intrigued by the attitudes about curiosity she kept bumping into that she wrote a cultural history of curiosity in the seventeenth and eighteenth centuries, titled simply, *Curiosity*.

In fact, says Benedict, before the Renaissance, official power, the kind of power that kings and queens had, along with the organization of society, and the limits on what you could ask questions about were all the same thing. They were interwoven.

Powerful people controlled information as well as armies. Rulers controlled the story.

In that setting, curiosity was a sin. It was a transgression. It was "an outlaw impulse," as Benedict described it in her book.[4] Curiosity, including scientific curiosity, was a challenge to the power structure of society—starting with the monarch himself. It was a challenge to two millennia of "wisdom"—"I'm the king because God said I should be the king. You are a serf because God said you should be a serf"—that culminated in the American Revolution.

Curiosity—asking questions—isn't just a way of understanding the world. It's a way of changing it. The people in charge have always known that, going all the way back to the Old Testament, and the myths of Greece and Rome.

In some places, curiosity is considered almost as dangerous today as it was in 1649. The Chinese government censors the entire Internet for a nation of 1.4 billion people, almost half of whom are online.[5]

And everywhere, curiosity retains a little aura of challenge and impertinence.

Consider what happens when you ask someone a question. They might respond, "That's a good question."

Or they might respond, "That's a curious question."

Often, the person who says, "That's a good question" has the answer ready—it's a good question, in part, because the person knows the answer. They may also genuinely think you've asked a good question—a question that has caused them to have a fresh thought.

The person who says, "That's a curious question," on the other hand, is feeling challenged. They either don't have an answer at hand, or they feel the question itself is somehow a challenge to their authority.

So why hasn't the Internet done more to usher in a wider golden age of curiosity?

I do think the questions we ask by typing them into an Internet search engine are a kind of curiosity. You can search the question, "Which is faster, a bee or a car?" and find a couple of helpful discussions.

But the Internet runs the risk, as Barbara Benedict puts it, of being turned into a more comprehensive version of the pope. It's simply a big version of "the machine with all the answers."

Yes, sometimes you simply need to know the GDP of the Ukraine or how many ounces are in a pint. We've always had great reference books for things like that—the *World Almanac* used to be a definitive source.

Those are facts.

But here's the really important question: does having all of human knowledge available in the palm of our hands make us more curious, or less curious?

When you read about the speed of bees flying, does that inspire you to learn more about the aerodynamics of bees—or does it do the opposite, does it satisfy you enough so you go back to Instagram?

It was Karl Marx who called religion "the opium of the masses."[6] He meant that religion was designed to provide enough answers that people stopped asking questions.

We need to be careful, individually, that the Internet doesn't anesthetize us instead of inspire us.

There are two things you can't find on the Internet—just like there were two things Robert Hooke couldn't find in the Bible or in the decrees of King Charles I:

You can't search for the answer to questions that haven't been asked yet.

And you can't Google a new idea.

The Internet can only tell us what we already know.

. . .

IN THE COURSE OF a business meeting, people in the movie business will often say, "That's good enough."

They'll say, "That script is good enough." "That actor is good enough." "That director is good enough."

When someone says to me, "That's good enough," it never is. It means exactly the opposite. It means the person, or the script, *isn't* good enough.

I'm sure the same thing happens in every line of work.

It's such an odd expression, that means exactly the opposite of what the words themselves mean. It's a way of saying, We're going to settle here. Mediocrity will do just fine.

I'm not interested in "good enough."

I think part of my reservoir of determination comes from all those decades of curiosity conversations with people who themselves didn't settle for "good enough." Their experiences, their accomplishments, are a reminder that you cannot live by curiosity alone. To have a satisfying life (and to make valuable use of curiosity), you also have to have discipline and determination. You have to apply your own imagination to what you learn. Most important, you have to treat the people around you with respect and with grace, and curiosity can help you do that.

For me, the most valuable kind of curiosity is the kind where there isn't a specific question I'm trying to get the answer to. The most valuable kind of curiosity is the truly openhearted question—whether to a Nobel laureate or the person sitting next to you at a wedding.

And I've come to realize over time that you archive curiosity—that is, you archive the results of your curiosity, you save up the insights and the energy it gives you.

There are a couple of ways of thinking about the kind of open-ended curiosity I've been so determined to pursue since I was in my twenties. Those conversations are like a mutual fund—a long-term investment in dozens of different people, personalities, specialties, themes. Some of them will be interesting at the moment we're having the conversation, but not afterward. Some of them aren't even interesting while we're doing them. And some of them will pay off hugely in the long term—because the conversation will spark a broad interest, and a deeper exploration, by me; or because the conversation will get tucked away, and a decade later an idea or an opportunity or a script will come along and I'll understand it completely, because of a conversation I had years before.

But just like with the stock market, you don't know in advance which conversations will perform, and which won't. So you just keep doing them—you invest a little bit of effort across a wide range of time, space, and people, confident that it's the right thing to do.

I also think of the conversations as an artist might. Artists are always watching for ideas, for points of view, for artifacts that might be helpful. An artist walking along the beach might find a dramatic piece of driftwood, eroded in an interesting way. The driftwood doesn't fit into any project the artist is working on right now; it's just compelling on its own. The smart artist takes the driftwood home, displays it on a shelf, and in a month or in a decade, the artist looks up, notices the driftwood again—and turns it into art.

I don't have any idea where good ideas come from, but I do know this:

The more I know about the world—the more I understand about how the world works, the more people I know, the more perspectives I have—the more likely it is that I'll have a good idea. The more likely it is that I'll understand a good idea when I hear it. The less likely I'll agree that something is "good enough."

When you know more, you can do more.

Curiosity is a state of mind. More specifically, it's the state of having an open mind. Curiosity is a kind of receptivity.

And best of all, there is no trick to curiosity.

You just have to ask one good question a day, and listen to the answer.

Curiosity is a more exciting way to live in the world. It is, truly, the secret to living a bigger life.

Brian Grazer's
Curiosity Conversations: A Sampler

As part of the work to write *A Curious Mind*, I did something I had never done before: assembled in one place as comprehensive a list as possible of the people I've had curiosity conversations with over the last thirty years. (Actually, some of the staff at Imagine did most of the work to create the list—for which I'm incredibly thankful.)

Looking through the list of people I've had the chance to talk to is, for me, like turning the pages of a photo album. Just like a single snapshot sometimes does, a name can trigger a wave of memories: where I was when I met that person, what we talked about, what they were wearing, even someone's posture, attitude, or facial expression.

Reading through the list over and over as we worked on the book, I was struck by two things. First, an incredible sense of gratitude that so many people agreed to sit and talk to me, to give me a sense of their world, when there wasn't anything tangible to be gained. All these years later, I wish I could call each of these people up and say thank you, again, for what they added to my life. Each person was an adventure—even if we were just sitting on the couches in my office—a journey well beyond the confines and routines of my own life. The breadth of experience and personality and accomplishment on the list is inspiring.

And second, although *A Curious Mind* is populated with stories from the conversations, we had so many more we didn't include that it seemed like it would be fun to offer a wider selection. What follows is a sampler—bonus material, we might call it here in Hollywood—from some of the curiosity conversations that have stayed with me.

Lunch with Fidel

The Hotel Nacional in Havana sits on the seaside boulevard, the Malecón, and it has two dozen rooms that are named after famous people who have stayed in them—Fred Astaire (room 228), Stan Musial (245), Jean Paul Sartre (539), and Walt Disney (445) are examples.

When I visited Havana in February 2001, I was put in the Lucky Luciano Suite (211), a pair of rooms named for the famous Mafioso that are really too large for one person.

I had come with a group of guy friends—we'd decided we wanted to do one guy trip a year, and we started with Cuba. (I tell a little bit of the story on pages 125–126). The Cuba trip was organized by Tom Freston, who was the CEO of MTV at the time, and the group included Brad Grey, the producer; Jim Wiatt, head of the talent agency William Morris; Bill Roedy, former head of MTV International, Graydon Carter, editor of *Vanity Fair*, and Leslie Moonves, CEO of CBS, including the CBS News division.

This was long before the thaw in relations between the United States and Cuba, of course, and a visit to Cuba in those days was a challenge—you never knew quite where you would get to go or whom you would get to meet.

Before we went to Cuba, I invested a lot of effort trying quietly to set up a curiosity conversation with Fidel Castro, without making any headway.

We flew into a Cuban military base—and it turned out that several of us had separately tried to set up meetings with Fidel. We made it clear to the folks taking care of us that we would welcome a meeting with Fidel.

Cubans, we learned during our visit, try to avoid referring to Fidel by name. They have a gesture they use in place of saying his name—you use your thumb and forefinger to pull on your chin like you're stroking a beard.

We had a few false alarms. Once we were leaving a Havana club at two thirty in the morning, and an aide came and told us Fidel would see us at four a.m.. We were exhausted. We all looked at each other and said, "Okay! Let's do it!"

Almost as soon as we said yes, word came back that the meeting wasn't going to happen after all.

The day before we left, we were told that Fidel would host us as a group for lunch the next day, starting at noon. We had been scheduled to leave then, so we had to push our departure back.

The next morning, we were ready to go. We were given a destination. We piled into the cars and headed off at high speed. Then, suddenly, the cars swerved to the side, did a U-turn, and accelerated in exactly the opposite direction, to a different destination.

Was that mystery? Theatrics? Was it designed to provide Fidel with some real security? Who knows.

As soon as we arrived at the new location, we were introduced to Fidel, who was dressed in his classic army fatigues. We were all given rum drinks, and we stood around talking.

I was with Les Moonves, talking to Fidel. Les was arguably the most powerful person in our group, and after William Paley himself (founder of CBS), he was arguably the most successful broadcaster of all time. Fidel clearly knew who Les was, and treated him as if he were the "leader" of our group, directing a lot of his attention to Moonves. Fidel talked with such energy that he actually had two translators, who took turns.

Fidel, too, held a drink, but in an hour of standing around, I never saw the glass touch his lips. I also never saw him tire, either of the standing or of holding the drink. After more than an hour, I whispered to Les, "Do you think we're ever going to go inside for lunch?"

Les said loudly, and partly to Fidel, "Maybe we ought to go inside and have lunch!"

As if he'd completely forgotten about the meal, Fidel agreed immediately and ushered us into lunch. The meal consisted of two parts: many long courses of Cuban food; and Fidel, talking about the wonders of Cuba. He didn't talk with us—he talked at us.

He knew the details of everything. The weather for every part of Cuba. The kilowatts required to run a light bulb in a Cuban home. He could granularize anything about the country, its people, its economy.

At one point, Fidel turned quite pointedly to Les and said, "When you get back to your country and your president, Bush, I wish you would tell him my thoughts"—and he proceeded to unfurl a long dissertation he wanted Moonves to pass on to the United States president. As if Les would naturally, and immediately, report in with President Bush.

For literally hours, Fidel didn't ask a single question of us, or engage us in conversation. He talked, and we ate and listened.

Finally, he paused. He looked at us. And then, through the translator, he said to me, "How do you get your hair to stand up that way?" Everybody laughed.

I think Fidel is so focused on symbolism and iconography that he might have been curious about what kind of statement I was trying to make with my hair. Feeling a little self-conscious, I decided to try to act smart. I said to Castro, "I make movies," and I listed the serious dramas we've made—only the dramas, none of the comedies—and I concluded by saying, "And I made a movie about how totalitarian governments torture their citizens, called *Closet Land*."

Clearly, I wasn't thinking at all. I guess I thought he would be impressed. Instead, maybe he thought, Perhaps we will detain the one with the funny hair for a year.

Graydon Carter looked at me with an expression that said, "Are you crazy?"

Then Graydon looked at Fidel, beamed, and said, "He also made *The Klumps!*"

It was the perfect deflection, but also scary. It gave me a moment to realize what I'd just said.

Fidel let it all pass without a raised eyebrow. Eventually, lunch stretched to five thirty. The jets were waiting to fly us back to the United States. Again, I nodded to Les that maybe it was time to go. And again, Les elegantly moved us along, telling Fidel it was really time for us to go.

Fidel presented each of us with a box of cigars as a parting gift. I was wearing a beautiful Cuban guayabera I had bought, and as we left, Fidel autographed the shirt, while I was wearing it, right in the middle of the back.

The Hero, the Prediction and the Dangerous Baseball Cap

On this particular day in June 2005, the second stop of the afternoon was a magnificent office in the United States Capitol. It was generously appointed, with rich wood paneling and solid, elegant furniture. The space conveyed not so much a sense of power as something much deeper: a sense of authority. It was the office of Senator John McCain, and I had an appointment to have a curiosity conversation with one of the most interesting and influential men in the United States Senate.

It was shaping up to be quite an afternoon, that Wednesday, June 8. I had spent the hour in one of the least regal Senate offices before arriving at McCain's office, with one of the least influential members of the United States Senate at the time: Barack Obama.

And after my conversation with Senator McCain, I had to hustle a few blocks up Pennsylvania Avenue to the White House to have dinner and a movie with the most powerful person in the world—President George W. Bush.

Obama. McCain. Bush. One-on-one, within the same four hours. That's about as amazing a lineup as one guy from outside Washington can have in a single afternoon inside the Beltway.

It happened because President Bush invited us to screen the movie *Cinderella Man* at the White House just as it opened in theaters. *Cinderella Man*, directed by Ron Howard, was inspired by the true-life story of Depression-era boxer James J. Braddock, who was played by Russell Crowe, with Renée Zellweger starring as his wife and Paul Giamatti as his manager.

I thought if I was going to go spend a couple days in Washington, it would be fun to see some people I was curious about.

For me, McCain was an obvious choice. His appeal is elemental: John McCain is a real American hero. He was a pilot in Vietnam, he was shot down, captured, and tortured; he survived and went on to become an important political figure. Even in the North Vietnam prison camps where he was held, McCain's fellow American prisoners regarded him as a leader. In the Senate and across the country in 2005, McCain had a reputation for smarts, independence, and determination.

The psychology and the character of heroes fascinate me— almost every movie we've made is about what it means to be a hero in some way or another.

But my meeting with McCain was oddly anti-climatic. We ended up talking not about substance but about oddly generic things—we talked about baseball, which I know very little about. We talked about the elderly.

McCain's presence was as impressive as his office. He was clearly in charge. He was polite to me, but I got the sense in the end that he wasn't quite sure what I was doing there. I was just a relatively well-known person on his schedule for an hour. One thing was clear: John McCain didn't have to worry about time, because everybody around him was paying attention to the time.

At one point in our conversation, his chief assistant came in and she said, "One minute, sir!" And I'm not kidding, sixty seconds later, that woman came back in and said, "You're up!"

Senator McCain rose. His jacket was already on, of course. He buttoned it as he stood, he shook my hand, and he was gone. A moment later, one of the aides pointed to the television in McCain's office—and there he was, striding onto the Senate floor.

.   .   .

IN CONTRAST TO MY previous conversation, meeting with Barack Obama couldn't have been more complete. Senator McCain had been in the Senate eighteen years, and just the last November he had been re-elected to his fourth term representing Arizona, with a stunning 77 percent of the vote. He was at the top of his influence, and rising.

Barack Obama had been in the United States Senate five months. Just a year earlier, Obama was still an Illinois State Senator.

But it was at the Democratic National Convention the previous summer—at the convention that nominated Senator John Kerry as the Democrat to challenge George W. Bush— that Barack Obama first came to the nation's attention, and mine as well. That's where Obama gave the galvanizing keynote address, with optimistic lines like "There's not a liberal America and a conservative America. There's the United States of America."

That day I met him for the first time, he was the only black United States Senator. He was also way down on the seniority list—like in the nineties. His office was number ninety-nine— the second least desirable. To get to Obama's office, we walked a long way, took the Capitol tram, then walked another long way.

When I arrived at his office, I was struck first by the number of people coming and going. It was in a basement, the light wasn't great. It was like some cross between a Saturday swap meet and the DMV. Obama's office was totally open, people were just coming and going, taking advantage of the chance to visit their senator.

There were a lot of fascinating people in the Senate I could have seen that afternoon, a lot of important people in Washington. Why had I asked for an appointment to see Obama, who was not even a significant senator, let alone a force on the national stage?

When I had seen Obama speak on television, like everybody who watched him, I was captivated and intrigued. To me, his communication skills were in another category. His communication skills were like Muhammad Ali's boxing skills. It seemed as if he were performing magic, rhetorical magic.

I'm in the communication business. My job is to make words into images, and have those images ignite emotions in the audience, emotions that are more forceful than the original words.

Obama, when I saw him speak, in the same way one might have seen Ali punch, was doing something beyond any other speaker I'd seen. He was igniting emotions with words—the same way an image could.

Obama's office was very humble, but he was very welcoming—and he was totally present. None of the distraction you often find with busy, important people who are with you, yet constantly checking the clock or their email, their minds in four other places at once. He's tall and wiry, and we sat on couches that were catty-corner—he greeted me, then he folded himself onto the couch with acrobatic fluidity, like an athlete would. He seemed completely relaxed, and totally comfortable with himself.

We talked about our families, we talked about work—it was more of a personal conversation than a policy conversation. While we talked, energetic young people—his staff—were constantly coming and going from the office, but he was undistracted.

Obama conveyed a real sense of confidence. He was in office number ninety-nine, but he was completely self-assured. Obama was just a year out of the Illinois State House, and five months into the Senate, and not even four years later he would be President of the United States.

As I was leaving Senate office number ninety-nine, I bumped into Jon Favreau, the talented writer who was working for Obama as a speechwriter. They had met at the Democratic National Convention, where Obama gave the keynote.

"If you ever decide to get out of politics," I said to Favreau half-jokingly, "and you want to work in Hollywood, give me a call. You're awesome."

"Thanks so much," said Favreau, smiling. "But I think he's going to want me."

. . .

I HADN'T TOLD Senator McCain and Senator Obama that I was going to see the other one. But I had told them both I was going to the White House that evening to screen *Cinderella Man* for President George W. Bush.

I'd met President Bill Clinton several times, and I was very intrigued by President Bush, and curious to see his style. President Bush's body language that evening was very different. When he's talking to you, it isn't face-to-face, or at least it wasn't when he spoke to me.

President Bush approached me, and we were introduced; he was very warm, very unpretentious. Then, as we started to talk, he sort of moved to my side, he put his arm around me—that's how he likes to talk, like two buddies, shoulder-to-shoulder. I liked that.

He did another thing that caught my attention. As the pre-movie food was being served, President Bush got a tray for himself, put his food on it, and then sat down at a table all alone. He didn't seem to need his folks around him. That table filled up, of course. But I thought that was pretty impressive. President Bush stayed for the whole movie.

The only disappointing part of the evening had to do with a small gift I had for President Bush. I brought him a ball cap from the TV show *Friday Night Lights*. President Bush grew up in Odessa, Texas, of course, and I thought he would get a kick out of it.

So I was standing in line to go through security at the White House gate, and I was so excited about the hat, so I showed it to the security officers. "The president is from Odessa, Texas, and I brought him this hat from *Friday Night Lights* as a gift," I said, "I'm going to give it to him."

I thought that would make everyone smile.

Boy was I wrong. They looked at me. They looked at the hat. They took the hat from me. They put it through a couple of different machines. A couple more people examined it, inside and out.

Then someone nodded and said to me, "You won't be handing the hat to the president. We'll give the hat to the president for you."

I would have been better off not saying anything, and just wearing the hat into the White House on my own head.

I never saw the hat again. I did tell President Bush about it—and I hope at some point someone handed it to him.

The Gloved One

In the early 1990s, I routinely tried to sit down with Michael Jackson. We would call his office a couple of times a year and ask for a meeting, invite him over. He wasn't interested.

Then, all of a sudden, he said yes. It wasn't clear why, although this was the period we were doing movies like *Parenthood* and *Kindergarten Cop* and *My Girl*, which were family-friendly, and I had heard that Jackson was interested in doing movies like that himself.

When the day arrived, his advance people came up to the office first. There was a lot of excitement—as you might imagine—and then Jackson appeared.

Jackson was already known at that point for those shy, slightly unusual gestures of his. But there was none of that. He seemed like a totally normal person—although he was wearing the gloves, the white gloves.

I was a Michael Jackson fan, of course—you couldn't follow music in America in the 1970s and 1980s and not be a fan of Michael Jackson. But I wasn't a crazed fan—so I wasn't particularly nervous. I respected Jackson, I thought he was an amazing talent.

He was about five feet nine inches tall—he was thin, but you could tell he was strong. He stepped into my office and sat down.

"What a pleasure to meet you," I said. "This is great."

He was acting normally, so I decided to treat him normally. I had the thought: I'm going to ask him to take off his gloves. Anyone normal coming in from outside would take off their gloves, right?

It could have been the end of the conversation right there.

But I didn't hesitate. I said, "Would you mind taking off your gloves?"

And he did. Simple as that. I thought, He took off the gloves—we're going to be okay.

Michael Jackson was clearly not much of a small-talk person. And to be honest, I didn't know exactly what to talk to him about. I certainly didn't want to bore him.

I asked, "How do you create music?"

And he immediately started to talk about how he creates music—how he composes it, how he performs it, all in a way that was almost scientific.

In fact, his whole manner transformed. When we first started talking, he had that high, slightly childish voice people know. But as soon as he started to talk about making music, even his voice changed, and he became another person—it was like a master class, like a professor from Julliard was talking. Melody, lyrics, what the mixing engineer does. It blew my mind.

We did talk a little bit about movies—Jackson had already done amazing videos, including the video for *Thriller*, which was directed by John Landis. It was a curiosity conversation with a touch of business about it.

Although I never met him again, there was nothing odd or uncomfortable about the hour we spent together. I came away with a very different impression of Michael Jackson. It made me feel like he wasn't so much a weird guy, or a collection of weird affectations—he was just someone who struggled with fame. The behavior was somehow environmental. I was so struck by the fact that I could talk to him like an adult, and he talked back like an adult.

I could ask him to take off the gloves, and he'd take off the gloves.

The Missed Opportunity

In some interesting ways, Andy Warhol had a lot in common with Michael Jackson. They both had a distinctive physical presence, a physical presence that each had consciously crafted for himself. They both did such impressive, influential work that simply saying either name conjures a whole style, a whole era. And they were both considered mysterious, enigmatic, almost impenetrable.

I went to meet Andy Warhol in the early 1980s, when I was visiting New York City, during a period when I had gotten the chance to meet a lot of artists, including David Hockney, Ed Ruscha, Salvador Dalí, and Roy Lichtenstein. By then, Andy Warhol had become an institution—he did the famous Campbell's soup can silk screens in 1962. I met him at his studio, The Factory. He was wearing his classic black turtleneck.

Two things were interesting to me about Warhol. The first is that he wasn't a brilliant technical artist—he didn't have the skills of, say, Roy Lichtenstein, and he wasn't trying to gain them. For him, the message of the art, the statement, was the most important thing.

And the second thing that was so striking when I met him in person was his absolute refusal to intellectualize his work. He almost didn't want to talk about it. He wasn't just understated. Every question brought the absolute simplest answer.

"Why did you do the portraits of Marilyn Monroe?" I asked.

"I like her," Warhol said.

We were strolling through The Factory, and there were silk screens everywhere, both finished and in progress.

"Why would you do your art on silk screens?" I asked.

"So we can make many of them," he said. Just like that—never an elaborate explanation.

Warhol had a reputation for being detached. During that visit to his studio, he was totally with me. He was a little trippy, in that sixties way. "Hey man, let's go over here," he would say.

And he was a little hard to talk to. But he was easy to hang out with.

I was back in New York City just a few weeks later, and I returned for a second visit.

He told me, "I'm going to go out to Los Angeles and do a *Love Boat* episode." I thought to myself, What's he talking about? Andy Warhol on *The Love Boat*—with Captain Stubing and Julie McCoy? I couldn't picture it. I thought he was kidding.

"I'm going to act in an episode of *The Love Boat*," Warhol said. I didn't realize he'd done those kinds of pop culture appearances before. He liked to surprise people. And he did it: He was on a *Love Boat* episode broadcast October 12, 1985, along with Milton Berle and Andy Griffith.

At that second meeting, Warhol said to me, "I didn't realize your partner is Ron Howard. He's Richie Cunningham!"

Warhol had an idea.

"I would love to take a picture of Ron Howard, and do two paintings—a before and an after. I want to take a picture of Ron Howard now, with his handlebar mustache, then I want to shave off the mustache, and I'll do another picture.

"Two of them. One with the mustache. One with no mustache. Before and after."

I thought immediately of Warhol's dual portraits of Elvis.

But I didn't mention that. I told Warhol I would talk to Ron about it.

I got back to LA and I said to Ron, "Andy Warhol wants to do this thing with you. He wants to do portraits of Ron Howard, before and after. He wants to shave off your mustache." I was pretty excited.

Ron wasn't excited, he was more baffled than anything. "You know, Brian, I don't really want to shave off my mustache," he said. "It's part of my identity now. I'm trying to get out of that 'American boy' identity."

Okay. I could understand that. Kind of. Not everybody has Andy Warhol asking to do portraits of them, of course. But I also knew how important Ron Howard's grown-up identity was to him—how important it's been to all of us, in fact.

So that was the end of Ron Howard, Before and After. Or so I thought.

Many years later, our movie *Cry-Baby* opened. As had become our habit, Ron Howard and I went to the Westwood Avco theater in Los Angeles on opening night to gauge the popularity of *Cry-Baby* firsthand. The Avco was the theater where there had been lines around the block for *Splash*. That Friday, to see *Cry-Baby*, there were seven people in a theater for five hundred.

Ron and I went home, had a couple of bottles of red wine, and watched *Drugstore Cowboy* to soften the disappointment. Ron had to catch a red-eye flight from LAX back east, so around 10 p.m. he headed out to the airport.

Before he flew out, he called me. He was a little buzzy. He

said, "Brian, I want you to know, I just went in the men's room here at the airport and shaved off my mustache."

And without thinking about it, I said, "Oh my God, you could have done that for Andy Warhol! Then we could have had two portraits of Ron Howard each worth fifty million."

These days, of course, Ron's mustache—in fact his full beard—is back. Ron is an icon without a Warhol silk screen.

Curiosity as Art

You probably know Jeff Koons's art. It's fun, it's outsized. He's done huge stainless steel sculptures in the shape of the balloon dogs that clowns make. He rendered an inflatable toy rabbit in the same vivid stainless steel, and it became so well-known that it was reproduced as a float in the Macy's Thanksgiving Day Parade.

To me, Koons's work is both exuberant and playful. It seems simple, too. But underneath is his rich understanding of history, of art theory.

I first met Jeff Koons twenty years ago, in the early 1990s. As with Warhol, I went to Koons's studio in New York. When you walk into his studio, knowing about the rabbit and the balloon dog, you think, I could do this. When you walk out after having spent a couple hours with Koons, you think, No one could duplicate what he's doing.

Although he worked on Wall Street as a commodities broker as a young man, Koons always wanted to be an artist. But he's not the kind of artist who bangs around his studio in blue jeans. He's more apt to dress like one of the great directors of the forties or fifties—like George Cukor or Cecil B. DeMille. In slacks and a nice shirt, fashionable and elegant.

He's a study in contrasts. Vocally, he's not loud. But his art and his actions are loud. For instance, in 1991, he married for the first time—to the famous Italian porn actress La Cicciolina. Then they did art together—including pictures in which they both appear naked, or mostly naked.

Koons is an unpretentious man, but he's willing to do risky, even shocking things on behalf of his art. And unlike Warhol, Koons is happy to talk to you about the sources of his art as well as its intellectual principles and historical perspective translated into visual form.

His studio, where he was producing all this dramatic art, felt almost like an expensive, elaborate science laboratory. It was almost antiseptic. He was like the calculating genius, the scientist, thinking and creating.

I went to his studio a second time much more recently—it was in a different place, and it was like the first studio, the science lab, had been taken to a whole new level.

Later, when we started talking about art for the cover of *A Curious Mind*, I suddenly thought of Jeff Koons. What would his approach to curiosity be? What would his approach to a book cover be?

I didn't ask him directly—I passed word through a mutual friend that I would love for him to do a drawing for the book. Word came back that he would definitely do it.

A month later, in the summer of 2014, we met at the Aspen Ideas Festival and I said to him, "I'm so excited you're doing a piece of art for the book!"

He said, "Tell me about the book."

I described the years of curiosity conversations, the people, the sense I have that I wouldn't have had anything like the kind of life I've had without curiosity. I told him that the point of the book is to inspire other people to see the simple power of curiosity to make their own lives better.

Koons's face lit up. "I understand," he said. "I love that."

And the drawing he did for the cover captures what we were talking about—a seemingly simple line drawing of a face that conveys exactly the joy, openheartedness, and excitement that being curious brings.

Writer Puts Producer in a Headlock

Perhaps the greatest boxing writer in modern America was Norman Mailer. He was a great writer about many things— Mailer won the National Book Award and two Pulitzers—and also a huge force in America's cultural landscape starting in the 1950s, when he cofounded *The Village Voice*.

When we started working on *Cinderella Man*, the boxing movie that we ultimately got to show to President Bush at the White House, I decided it would be fun and valuable to talk to Mailer about the boxer Jim Braddock and the role of boxing in Depression-era America.

I met Mailer in New York City in 2004. I let him pick the

place—he chose the Royalton Hotel, one of those famous old Midtown hotels that had once been elegant but was a little past its prime. (The Royalton has since been renovated.)

It was the kind of lobby that had those old lumpy couches covered with velvet. Slightly uncomfortable. We sat catty-corner to each other. Mailer sat very close to me.

When we met, he was eighty-one years old, but there was nothing old about him. We sat on the couches and talked about boxing, about our relationships. We complained to each other about our relationships.

Even at eighty-one, Mailer was a tough guy. He was short, and thick, and very strong. He had a big, tough face. And he had a very interesting voice. He enunciated every word. Every word had drama to it. You leaned into his voice.

It was about three in the afternoon, but Mailer ordered a drink. I remember thinking it was a little early to start drinking—but probably not in the world Norman Mailer lived and wrote in. He was a bridge to the era of Hemingway. He had something you'd expect from a guy like Mailer—something old-fashioned, like a sidecar. A whiskey drink.

Mailer liked the idea of a movie about Jim Braddock. He was crabby—he was crabby about most things that afternoon. But he liked the idea of the movie.

He was kind of funny. We took some pictures—he was willing to take pictures with me, but he wasn't warm and fuzzy about it. "Okay, take it. You've got a second to do it," he said.

When he was talking about boxing, he used his fists to

show the punches. He talked about individual fights—he could remember the sequence of punches in specific rounds in specific fights—and he showed me the punches, he literally did the punches. He talked about the physiognomy of the boxers, how they study each other's bodies and faces, looking for the places where the punches will really hurt.

He was demonstrating an exchange of punches in a particular fight, and he said, "And then he threw him out of the ring."

I was surprised. I asked, "How'd that go? How did he throw him out of the ring?"

He just reached over, said "It went like this," and then all of a sudden Norman Mailer had me in a headlock. Right in the lobby of the Royalton Hotel. The famous writer put the Hollywood producer in a headlock.

I wasn't quite sure what to do.

With his arms wrapped around my head, it was clear how strong he was. It was slightly embarrassing. I didn't want to struggle. But I also wasn't quite sure what would happen next. How long would Mailer keep me in the headlock?

It lasted long enough to leave a strong impression.

Breakfast with Oprah

I got to meet Oprah Winfrey at just the moment when I needed to meet her. I was feeling a little low, and Oprah was exactly the kind of warm, reflective, and honest person I needed to talk to.

It was early 2007. I had never crossed paths with Oprah, despite all her impact on TV and the movies.

I was talking to Spike Lee, and I knew they were friends. "I want more than anything to meet Oprah," I said to Spike. "Will you help me?"

Spike laughed. "Just call her, man!" he said.

"I don't know her," I said. "I don't think she'll call me back."

Spike laughed again. "She knows who you are," he said. "Just call her."

Spike gave me the push I needed. I called Oprah.

The next day, I was sitting in my office, meeting with Jennifer Lopez. In fact, JLo was in the office singing a beautiful Spanish ballad for me.

My assistant knocked on the door, cracked it open, and said in a stage whisper: "Oprah's on the phone. It's Oprah herself."

I winced. I looked at Jennifer. I said, "JLo, it's Oprah herself. I have to talk to her. Let me take that call."

Jennifer graciously stopped singing. But she wasn't smiling.

I picked up the phone. "Oprah!" I said. "I can't begin to tell you how much I'd like to meet you. I'll go wherever you are." I explained my curiosity meetings in just a sentence.

And in that wonderfully reassuring Oprah voice, she said, "I'm happy to meet you, Brian. Of course I know who you are." And then she said something nice about one of my movies.

"I'm going to be at the Bel-Air Hotel in LA in just a couple of days," she added.

And that's how I came to be sitting outside ten days later, on the morning of January 29, 2007, in the courtyard of the Bel-Air Hotel in Los Angeles, waiting to have breakfast with Oprah Winfrey.

I was feeling low because I was going through a relationship crisis. I had to make a major life choice.

Oprah came down to breakfast with her friend and colleague Gayle King. We had huevos rancheros. We talked about life, about relationships, about what is really important and how to hold on to it—not just in the moment, but in the long term.

Who better to have that kind of conversation with when you're feeling emotionally bruised and uncertain?

Oprah has that deep well of common-sense wisdom. Oprah also knows how to listen. She reminded me that life is the process itself, not the individual moments—that there's fallibility, that of course there is both happiness and unhappiness.

"I'm always trying to solve life myself," she said.

We talked for almost two hours. It became evident that Oprah had a lot of things she had to attend to. Gayle was ready—she was dressed in a business suit. Oprah, on the other hand, had to go back to her room to get ready to tackle her day. She'd come to the poolside breakfast wearing her pajamas. And that was exactly the comfort level of our conversation—as if we'd both been wearing pajamas.

Sharing a Bowl of Ice Cream with a Princess

For pure excitement, nothing quite tops a real prince and princess. In September 1995, we were invited to do a Royal Premiere of the movie *Apollo 13* in London for Prince Charles and Princess Diana and the Royal Family.

The way a Royal Premiere works is a little different than, for instance, the White House showings we do. You meet the Royals at a movie theater in London, and then, in the case of *Apollo 13*, everyone is invited to dinner afterward at a different location.

Prince Charles and Princess Di had already formally separated, so we weren't quite sure who would come to the event. But as soon as we knew it was going to happen, I violated protocol by reaching out to the office of Princess Diana. I explained that I looked forward to the premiere, and to meeting Her Royal Highness, and that I did these curiosity meetings, and that I would welcome the chance to sit down one-on-one with the Princess either before or after the evening's events.

Perhaps not surprisingly, I didn't hear anything back.

The premiere went off September 7 at a theater in London's West End, and we all lined up to formally greet Princess Diana (Prince Charles did not attend). After the movie, several dozen of us adjourned to dinner at a big restaurant with long rectangular tables. We all took our seats, as instructed.

Now, when you do a Royal Premiere, before you even get on the plane to cross the Atlantic Ocean, the folks from Universal Studios come and brief you on the protocol for being in the presence of members of the Royal Family: how to greet them ("Your Royal Highness"), that you don't touch them, the moments when you should stand and when you should sit and when you should bow. You get a second briefing after you arrive in London.

So we took our seats for dinner, and the last person to walk in was Princess Diana. As she entered, everyone stood up. She sat, and we took our seats—and sitting directly across from me was Princess Diana.

Without being told, it seemed like I was going to get my curiosity conversation after all.

Diana was extremely beautiful—in fact, that night, Princess Diana was wearing a short black Versace dress that got a lot of notice in the London press as being perhaps the shortest dress she'd ever worn in public.

As soon as she sat down, I made a decision in my mind: I was not going to let our conversation conform to the stilted style that protocol would dictate.

I decided to be funny, to be jokey. She connected immediately—she joked right back. You could tell people around her were a little surprised at my behavior, and at her playful participation.

She did love *Apollo 13*. She didn't get animated like I would. With that wonderful British lilt, she said, "It was a tremendous film. Really, triumphant. An important movie."

Over dinner, we talked about movies. We talked about pop culture in America. Tom Hanks was sitting on one side of the

Princess, and he was in very funny form himself that evening. Ron Howard was on the other side of the Princess. I'd say between Tom and me trying to make the Princess laugh, I'm not sure Ron got the chance to talk very much.

Diana reminded me of Audrey Hepburn in the movie *Roman Holiday*—although in Diana's case, she was the ordinary person who became a princess, instead of the other way around. Diana's charisma came from her beauty, her poise, her attentiveness.

I was most surprised by her sense of humor. I didn't expect her to laugh at our jokes. I thought she would smile—but she laughed. It seemed liberating. She was the most famous person in the world, but also a little trapped. The laughter was a touch of freedom.

At dinner, there was no ordering—the menu had been set in advance. As we were finishing the main course, I said to the Princess, "You know, I really like ice cream. Do you think I could get some ice cream?"

Princess Diana smiled. "If you want some ice cream," she said, "why don't you order some from one of the waiters?"

I called a waiter over and said, "I was wondering if the Princess and I could share a bowl of ice cream."

Princess Diana looked at me with an expression that seemed to say, "That was cute. That was ballsy. And I'm a little aghast."

The waiters scrambled to get ice cream. I'd say I've never seen waiters scramble around quite like they did trying to find that ice cream, in fact.

Shortly, a bowl of ice cream was presented to me—a scoop of chocolate and a scoop of vanilla. Naturally, I offered the bowl to Princess Diana first, and she took a spoonful or two. Then I had some.

Then before it was all gone, I offered the bowl back to Princess Diana. And although I'd been eating from it, she took several more bites. She ate after me. That sort of stunned me. She was smiling.

Then, all of a sudden, the Princess had to leave.

I said, "Why do you have to leave? We're having such a good time!"

She said, "It's protocol. I have to leave before midnight." Just like in a fairy tale.

Then the Princess stood, and we all stood, and she was gone.

Brian Grazer's
Curiosity Conversations: A List

Since the late 1970s, Brian Grazer has been meeting with people from diverse backgrounds to have open-ended conversations about their lives and work. Below, in alphabetical order, is a list of many of the people Brian has had curiosity conversations with. It is as comprehensive as memory and records permit; please forgive any omissions. Brian has spoken to so many people over thirty-five years and explored so many topics that it would be impossible to have included accounts of all of them. But each of the conversations provided the inspiration for the discussions of creativity and storytelling in this book, and in Brian's work.

50 Cent: musician, actor, entrepreneur
Joan Abrahamson: president of the research and education non-profit Jefferson Institute, MacArthur Fellowship recipient
Paul Neal "Red" Adair: oil-well firefighter, innovator in extinguishing oil-well blowouts in Kuwait

Roger Ailes: president of Fox News Channel

Doug Aitken: multimedia artist

Muhammad Ali: professional heavyweight boxer, three-time World Heavyweight Champion

John Allman: neuroscientist, expert on human cognition

Gloria Allred: civil rights attorney

Brad Anderson: former CEO of Best Buy

Chris Anderson: curator of TED conferences

Philip Anschutz: entrepreneur, cofounder of Major League Soccer, investor in multiple professional sports teams

David Ansen: former senior entertainment editor at *Newsweek*

Rose Apodaca: pop culture, fashion, and style journalist

Bernard Arnault: chairman and CEO of LVMH

Rebecca Ascher-Walsh: journalist, author

Isaac Asimov: science fiction author

Reza Aslan: scholar of religious studies, author

Tony Attwood: psychologist, author of books on Asperger's syndrome

Lesley Bahner: responsible for advertising and motivational research for the Reagan-Bush 1984 presidential campaign

F. Lee Bailey: legendary defense attorney who represented Patricia Hearst and Sam Sheppard

Evan Bailyn: expert on search-engine optimization, author of *Outsmarting Google*

Letitia Baldrige: etiquette expert, Jacqueline Kennedy's social secretary

Bob Ballard: oceanographer, explorer, underwater archeologist who discovered the *Titanic*

David Baltimore: biologist, Nobel laureate

Richard Bangs: explorer, author, TV personality

Tyra Banks: model, TV host

Barry Barish: experimental physicist, expert on gravitational waves

Colette Baron-Reid: expert on intuition

John C. Beck: business expert in mobile communications, author

Yves Béhar: industrial designer, entrepreneur, sustainability advocate

Harold Benjamin: director of the Wellness Community centers for cancer patients

Steve Berra: professional skateboarder, cofounder of popular skateboarding website The Berrics

Jeff Bewkes: CEO and chairman of Time Warner

Jeff Bezos: founder and CEO of Amazon.com, owner of the *Washington Post*

Jason Binn: founder of *DuJour* magazine, chief advisor to Gilt Groupe, editor of Getty WireImage

Ian Birch: director of editorial development and special projects at Hearst Magazines, former editor of *US* magazine

Peter Biskind: cultural critic, film historian, author, former executive editor of *Premiere* magazine

Edwin Black: historian and journalist focusing on human rights and corporate abuse

Keith Black: chairman of neurosurgery at Cedars-Sinai Medical Center, Los Angeles, specializing in the treatment of brain tumors

David Blaine: magician, illusionist, endurance artist

Keith Blanchard: founding editor of *Maxim*

Alex Ben Block: journalist, former senior editor of the *Hollywood Reporter*

Sherman Block: sheriff of Los Angeles County, 1982–1998

Michael Bloomberg: mayor of New York City, 2002–2013, founder of Bloomberg financial information service

Tim Blum: cofounder of contemporary commercial art gallery Blum & Poe

Adam Bly: creator of *Seed* magazine, which focused on the intersection of science and society

Alex Bogusky: designer, advertising executive, marketer, author

David Boies: attorney who represented U.S. Justice Department in *U.S. v. Microsoft* and Al Gore in *Bush v. Gore*

Mark Borovitz: rabbi, ex-convict who runs a residential treatment center for ex-convicts and drug addicts

Anthony Bozza: music journalist and author, writer for *Rolling Stone*

William Bratton: police commissioner of New York City

Eli Broad: philanthropist, entrepreneur, art collector

John Brockman: literary agent, author, founder of the Edge Foundation

Bradford Brown: translator of *The Book of Five Rings*, a book written by a Japanese samurai on the art of confrontation and victory

Roy Brown: musician, composer

Tim Brown: CEO and president of design firm IDEO

Willie Brown: former mayor of San Francisco who served fifteen years as Speaker of the California State Assembly

Tiffany Bryan: contestant on reality TV show *Fear Factor*

Jane Buckingham: expert on forecasting trends

Ted Buffington: expert on performance under pressure and on decision making in critical situations

Vincent Bugliosi: deputy Los Angeles district attorney who prosecuted Charles Manson, cowrote *Helter Skelter*

Ed Bunker: career criminal and author of crime fiction

Tory Burch: fashion designer

James Burke: CEO of Johnson & Johnson during the 1982 Tylenol crisis

Cara-Beth Burnside: pioneer of women's skateboarding and snowboarding

Chandler Burr: journalist, author, curator of olfactory art at the Museum of Art and Design in New York City

Eugenia Butler, Sr.: art dealer and collector

James T. Butts, Jr.: mayor of Inglewood, former police chief of Santa Monica

David Byrne: musician, founding member of the band Talking Heads

Naomi Campbell: actress, supermodel

Adam Carolla: podcaster, former host of syndicated radio call-in program *Loveline*

John Carroll: journalist, former editor of the *Los Angeles Times* and the *Baltimore Sun*

Sean B. Carroll: evolutionary development biologist, geneticist

Mr. Cartoon: tattoo and graffiti artist

Carlos Castaneda: anthropologist, author of books describing his shamanism training

Celerino Castillo III: DEA agent who revealed the CIA-backed arms-for-drugs trade in Nicaragua

Brian Chesky: cofounder and CEO of Airbnb

Deepak Chopra: author, physician, alternative medicine advocate

Michael Chow: restaurateur

Chuck D: musician, music producer, former leader of Public Enemy

Steve Clayton: research futurist for Microsoft

Eldridge Cleaver: leader of the Black Panther Party, author of *Soul on Ice*

Johnnie Cochran: defense attorney who represented O. J. Simpson

Jared Cohen: director of Google Ideas

Joel Cohen: population specialist, mathematical biologist

Kat Cohen: university admissions counselor, author of *The Truth About Getting In*

William Colby: CIA director, 1973–1976

Elizabeth Baron Cole: nutritionist

Jim Collins: management consultant, expert on business and management, author of *Good to Great*

Robert Collins: neurologist, former chairman of neurology at UCLA School of Medicine

Sean Combs: musician, music producer, fashion designer, entrepreneur

Richard Conniff: author who specializes in human and animal behavior

Tim Cook: CEO of Apple, Inc.

Tatiana Cooley-Marquardt: repeat winner of USA Memory Championship

Anderson Cooper: journalist, author, TV personality, anchor of CNN's *Anderson Cooper 360*

Norman Cousins: medical guru, author of *Anatomy of an Illness: As Perceived by the Patient*

Jacques Cousteau: oceanographer, pioneered marine conservation

Chris W. Cox: chief lobbyist for the National Rifle Association

Steve Coz: former editor of *National Enquirer*

Donald Cram: professor of chemistry at UCLA, Nobel laureate in chemistry

Jim Cramer: investor, author, TV personality, host of CNBC's *Mad Money*

Clyde Cronkhite: criminal justice expert, former police chief of Santa Ana, former deputy police chief of Los Angeles

Mark Cuban: investor, owner of the NBA's Dallas Mavericks

Heidi Siegmund Cuda: journalist, former music critic for the *Los Angeles Times*

Thomas Cummings: leading expert in designing high-performing organizations and strategic change at USC Marshall School of Business

Fred Cuny: disaster relief specialist

Mario Cuomo: governor of New York, 1983–1994

Alan Dershowitz: attorney, constitutional scholar, professor emeritus at Harvard Law School

Donny Deutsch: advertising executive, TV personality

Jared Diamond: evolutionary biologist, author, professor at UCLA, winner of the Pulitzer Prize

Alfred "Fred" DiSipio: record promoter investigated during payola scandal

DMX: musician, actor

Thomas R. Donovan: former CEO of the Chicago Board of Trade

Jack Dorsey: cofounder of Twitter, founder and CEO of Square Inc.

Steve Drezner: specialist in systems analysis and military projects for RAND Corporation

Ann Druyan: author and producer specializing in cosmology and popular science

Marian Wright Edelman: founder and president of the Children's Defense Fund

Betty Edwards: author of *Drawing on the Right Side of the Brain*

Peter Eisenhardt: astronomer, physicist at NASA's Jet Propulsion Laboratory

Paul Ekman: psychologist, pioneer in the study of emotions and their relation to facial expressions

Anita Elberse: professor of business administration at Harvard Business School

Eminem: musician, music producer, actor

Selwyn Enzer: futurist, former director of USC Center for Futures Research

Susan Estrich: lawyer, author, first female campaign manager of a major presidential campaign (for Michael Dukakis)

Harold Evans: journalist, author, former editor of the *Sunday Times,* founded *Condé Nast Traveler*

Ron W. Fagan: sociologist, former professor at Pepperdine University

Barbara Fairchild: editor of *Bon Appétit*, 2000–2010

Shepard Fairey: artist, graphic designer, illustrator

Linda Fairstein: author, former chief prosecutor of the sex crimes unit for the Manhattan district attorney's office

John Fiedler: director of communications research for the 1984 Reagan-Bush presidential campaign

Louis C. Finch: former deputy undersecretary of defense for personnel and readiness for the U.S. Department of Defense

Henry Finder: editorial director of the *New Yorker*

Ted Fishman: journalist, author of *China, Inc.: How the Rise of the Next Superpower Challenges America and the World*

John Flicker: former president and CEO of the National Audubon Society

William Ford, Jr.: chairman and former CEO of the Ford Motor Company and great-grandson of Henry Ford

Matthew Freud: head of Freud Communications and great-grandson of Sigmund Freud

Glen Friedman: photographer who does a lot of work with skateboarders and musicians, artist, author of *Fuck You Heroes*

Bonnie Fuller: journalist, media executive, editor of HollywoodLife .com

Bob Garcia: baseball card collector and expert

Howard Gardner: developmental psychologist, developed theory of multiple intelligences

Daryl F. Gates: police chief of Los Angeles, 1978–1992

Vince Gerardis: entrepreneur

David Gibson: philosopher, scholar of ancient Greek philosopher Plato

Françoise Gilot: painter, author of *Life with Picasso*

Malcolm Gladwell: author, journalist, staff writer at the *New Yorker*

Rebecca Glashow: digital media executive involved in launching first video-on-demand system

Sheldon Glashow: theoretical physicist, professor emeritus at Harvard University, Nobel laureate in physics

Bernard Glassman: Zen teacher and cofounder of the Zen Peacemaker Order

Barry Glassner: president of Lewis & Clark College, former executive vice provost at the University of Southern California

John Goddard: adventurer, author, first man to kayak the entire Nile River

Russell Goldsmith: CEO of City National Bank

Adam Gopnik: staff writer for the *New Yorker* and author of *Paris to the Moon*

Andrew Gowers: former editor of the *Financial Times*

Robert Graham: sculptor

Brian Greene: theoretical physicist, professor at Columbia University, specialist in string theory

Robert Greene: author and speaker known for books on strategy, power, and seduction

Linda Greenhouse: journalist, former U.S. Supreme Court reporter for the *New York Times,* winner of the Pulitzer Prize

Lisa Gula: former scientist, working on missile defense systems at XonTech

Sanjay Gupta: neurosurgeon, chief medical correspondent for CNN

Ramón A. Gutiérrez: professor of history at the University of Chicago, specializing in U.S. race and ethnic relations

Joseph T. Hallinan: journalist, author, winner of the Pulitzer Prize for investigative reporting

Dean Hamer: geneticist, scientist emeritus at the National Cancer Institute, specializing in how genes affect human behavior

Dian Hanson: editor of pornographic magazines, editor for Taschen art books

Tom Hargrove: agricultural scientist who was kidnapped in Colombia by FARC narco-guerrillas, inspired the movie *Proof of Life*

Mark Harris: journalist, former executive editor of *Entertainment Weekly*

Sam Harris: neuroscientist, author of *The End of Faith*

Bill Harrison: vision specialist focusing on sports vision training to maximize eye-mind-body reflexes

Reed Hastings: cofounder and CEO of Netflix

Laura Hathaway: national coordinator for American Mensa International, Gifted Children Resource Programs

Zahi Hawass: archaeologist, Egyptologist, former minister of state for antiquities affairs in Egypt

John Hay: Freemason

Lutfallah Hay: former member of parliament in prerevolutionary Iran, Freemason

Susan Headden: former reporter and editor at *U.S. News & World Report*, winner of the Pulitzer Prize for investigative reporting

Jack Healey: human rights activist, former executive director of Amnesty International USA

Thomas Heaton: seismologist, professor at California Institute of Technology, contributed to the development of earthquake early warning systems

Peter Herbst: journalist, former editor of *Premiere* and *New York* magazines

Danette Herman: talent executive for Academy Awards

Seymour Hersh: investigative reporter, author, winner of the Pulitzer Prize for uncovering the My Lai massacre and its cover-up during the Vietnam War

Dave Hickey: art and cultural critic who has written for *Harper's*, *Rolling Stone*, and *Vanity Fair*

Jim Hightower: progressive political activist, radio talk-show host

Tommy Hilfiger: fashion designer, founder of lifestyle brand

Christopher Hitchens: journalist and author who was a critic of politics and religion

David Hockney: artist and major contributor to the Pop art movement in the 1960s

Nancy Irwin: hypnotherapist

Chris Isaak: musician, actor

Michael Jackson: singer, songwriter, his 1982 album *Thriller* is the bestselling album of all time

LeBron James: NBA basketball player

Mort Janklow: literary agent, founder and chairman of the literary agency Janklow & Nesbit Associates

Jay Z: musician, music producer, fashion designer, entrepreneur

Wyclef Jean: musician, actor

James Jebbia: CEO of the Supreme clothing brand

Harry J. Jerison: paleoneurologist, professor emeritus at UCLA

Steve Jobs: cofounder and former CEO of Apple Inc., cofounder and former CEO of Pixar

Betsey Johnson: fashion designer

Jamie Johnson: documentary filmmaker who directed *Born Rich*, heir to Johnson & Johnson fortune

Larry C. Johnson: former analyst for the CIA, security and terrorism consultant

Robert L. Johnson: businessman, media magnate, cofounder and former chairman of BET

Sheila Johnson: cofounder of BET, first African American woman to be an owner/partner in three professional sports teams

Steve Johnson: media theorist, popular science author, cocreated online magazine *FEED*

Jackie Joyner-Kersee: Olympic gold medalist, track star

Paul Kagame: president of Rwanda

Michiko Kakutani: book critic for the *New York Times,* winner of the Pulitzer Prize for criticism

Sam Hall Kaplan: former architecture critic for the *Los Angeles Times*

Masoud Karkehabadi: wunderkind who graduated from college at age thirteen

Patrick Keefe: author, staff writer for the *New Yorker*

Gershon Kekst: founder of the corporate communications company Kekst and Co.

Jill Kelleher: professional matchmaker and founder and CEO of Kelleher & Associates

Robin D. G. Kelley: historian and professor at UCLA, specializing in African American studies

Sheila Kelley: actress and dancer, founder of S Factor pole dancing workout

Philip Kellman: cognitive psychologist and professor at UCLA, specializing in perceptual learning and adaptive learning

Joseph Kennedy II: businessman, Democratic politician, founder of Citizens Energy Corp., son of Sen. Robert F. Kennedy and Ethel Kennedy

Gayle King: editor-at-large for *O, The Oprah Magazine,* coanchor of *CBS This Morning*

Alex Kipman: technical fellow at Microsoft, coinventor of Kinect for Xbox

Robert Kirby: kinesiologist who studies the science of muscular medicine

Henry Kissinger: former U.S. secretary of state, diplomat, Nobel Peace Prize laureate

Calvin Klein: fashion designer

Elsa Klensch: journalist, fashion critic, former host of CNN's *Style with Elsa Klensch*

Phil Knight: cofounder, chairman, and former CEO of Nike Inc.

Beyoncé Knowles: musician, actress

Christof Koch: neuroscientist and professor at California Institute of Technology, specializing in human consciousness

Clea Koff: forensic anthropologist who worked with United Nations to reveal genocide in Rwanda

Stephen Kolodny: attorney; practices family law

Rem Koolhaas: architect, architectural theorist, professor at Harvard Graduate School of Design

Jeff Koons: artist

Jesse Kornbluth: journalist, editor of a cultural concierge service

Richard Koshalek: former director of the Museum of Contemporary Art, Los Angeles

Mark Kostabi: artist, composer

Anna Kournikova: former professional tennis player

Lawrence Krauss: theoretical physicist, cosmologist, professor at Arizona State University

Steve Kroft: journalist, correspondent for CBS's *60 Minutes*

William LaFleur: author, professor at the University of Pennsylvania, specializing in Japanese culture

Steven Lamy: professor of international relations at the University of Southern California

Lawrence Lawler: former special agent in charge of the Los Angeles field office of the FBI

Nigella Lawson: journalist, author, food writer, TV host

Sugar Ray Leonard: professional boxer who won world titles in five weight divisions

Maria Lepowsky: anthropologist, professor at University of Wisconsin–Madison, lived with the indigenous people of a Papua New Guinea island

Lawrence Lessig: activist for Internet freedom and Net neutrality, professor at Harvard Law School

Cliff Lett: professional race car driver, designer of radio-controlled cars

Robert A. Levine: former economist at RAND Corporation

Ariel Levy: journalist, staff writer at *New York* magazine

Dany Levy: founder of DailyCandy email newsletter

Roy Lichtenstein: Pop artist

John Liebeskind: former professor at UCLA, leading researcher in the study of pain and its relation to health

Alan Lipkin: former special agent for the criminal investigation division of the IRS

Margaret Livingstone: neurobiologist specializing in vision, professor at Harvard Medical School

Tone Lōc: musician, actor

Elizabeth Loftus: cognitive psychologist and expert on human memory, professor at the University of California, Irvine

Lisa Love: West Coast director for *Vogue* and *Teen Vogue*

Jim Lovell: Apollo-era astronaut, commander of the crippled Apollo 13 mission

Thomas Lovejoy: ecologist, professor at George Mason University, former assistant secretary for environmental and external affairs at the Smithsonian Institution, expert in tropical deforestation

Malcolm Lucas: chief justice of the California Supreme Court, 1987–1996

Oliver Luckett: founder and CEO of social media content company theAudience

Frank Luntz: political consultant and pollster

Peter Maass: author and journalist who covers international affairs, war, and conflict

Norman Mailer: author, playwright, filmmaker, journalist, cofounder of the *Village Voice*

Sir John Major: prime minister of the United Kingdom, 1990–1997

Michael Malin: astronomer, designer, developer of cameras used to explore Mars

P. J. Mara: former Irish senator and political adviser to Irish prime minister Charles Haughey

Lou Marinoff: philosopher who works with decision theory and political philosophy, professor at the City College of New York

Thom Mayne: architect, cofounder of architecture firm Morphosis

John McCain: U.S. senator from Arizona, Republican nominee for president in 2008

Terry McAuliffe: governor of Virginia, former chairman of the Democratic National Committee

Kevin McCabe: economic theorist, neuroeconomist, professor at George Mason University

Susan McCarthy: former city manager for Santa Monica

Susan McClary: musicologist who combines musicology with feminist music criticism, professor at Case Western Reserve University

Terry McDonell: editor, media executive, former editor in chief of *Esquire*

Paul McGuinness: former manager of the band U2

Robert McKee: creative writing instructor, former professor at the University of Southern California

Daniel McLean: classics scholar and lecturer at UCLA

Bruce McNall: sports executive, former owner of the National Hockey League's Los Angeles Kings

Leonard Mehlmauer: naturopath, researcher who created the term "eyology"

Sonny Mehta: chairman and editor in chief of Alfred A. Knopf publishing company

Steven Meisel: fashion photographer

Susan Meiselas: documentary photographer

Suzy Menkes: British journalist, author, former fashion reporter and editor for the *International Herald Tribune*

Millard "Mickey" Drexler: CEO and chairman of J. Crew, former president and CEO of the Gap

Jack Miles: editor, author, Pulitzer Prize winner, MacArthur Fellowship recipient

Marvin Mitchelson: celebrity divorce attorney, pioneered the concept of palimony

Isaac Mizrahi: fashion designer

Tim Montgomery: Olympic runner stripped of his world record after being found guilty of using performance-enhancing drugs

Robert Morgenthau: lawyer, longest-serving district attorney of Manhattan

Patrick B. Moscaritolo: CEO of Greater Boston Convention & Visitors Bureau

Kate Moss: supermodel, fashion designer

Lawrence Moulter: former chairman and CEO of the New Boston Garden Corporation

Bill Moyers: journalist, political commentator, former White House press secretary

Robert Mrazek: author, former congressman

Patrick J. Mullany: former special agent for the FBI, pioneered FBI's offender profiling

Kary Mullis: biochemist, Nobel laureate in chemistry for his work with DNA

Takashi Murakami: artist, painter, sculptor

Blake Mycoskie: entrepreneur, philanthropist, founder and chief shoe giver of TOMS shoes

Nathan Myhrvold: former chief technology officer at Microsoft

Ed Needham: former managing editor of *Rolling Stone* and editor in chief of *Maxim*

Sara Nelson: cofounder of the public interest law firm Christic Institute

Benjamin Netanyahu: prime minister of Israel

Jack Newfield: journalist, author, former columnist for the *Village Voice*

Nobuyuki "Nobu" Matsuhisa: chef and restaurateur

Peggy Noonan: speechwriter and special assistant to President Ronald Reagan, author, columnist for the *Wall Street Journal*

Anthony Norvell: expert on metaphysics, author

Barack Obama: president of the United States, former U.S. senator from Illinois

ODB: musician, music producer, founding member of Wu-Tang Clan

Richard Oldenburg: former director of the Museum of Modern Art, New York City

Mary-Kate and Ashley Olsen: actresses, fashion designers

Olu Dara & Jim Dickinson: musicians, record producers

Estevan Oriol: photographer whose work often depicts Los Angeles urban and gang culture

Lawrence Osborne: journalist, author of *American Normal: The Hidden World of Asperger Syndrome*

Manny Pacquiao: professional boxer, first eight-division world champion

David Pagel: art critic, author, curator, professor of art history at Claremont College specializing in contemporary art

Anthony Pellicano: high-profile private investigator in Los Angeles

Robert Pelton: conflict-zone journalist, author of *The World's Most Dangerous Places* books

Andy Pemberton: former editor in chief of *Blender* magazine

David Petraeus: director of the CIA, 2011–2012, retired four-star U.S. Army general

Mariana Pfaelzer: United States federal circuit court judge, opposed California's Proposition 187

Jay Phelan: evolutionary biologist, professor at UCLA

Ann Philbin: director of the Hammer Museum of Art, Los Angeles

Mark Plotkin: ethnobotanist, author, expert on rainforest ecosystems

Christopher "moot" Poole: Internet entrepreneur, created 4chan and Canvas websites

Peggy Post: director of the Emily Post Institute, author and consultant on etiquette

Virginia Postrel: political and cultural journalist, author

Colin Powell: U.S. secretary of state, 2001–2005, former chairman of the Joint Chiefs of Staff, former national security advisor, retired four-star U.S. Army general

Ned Preble: former executive, Synectics creative problem-solving methodology

Ilya Prigogine: chemist, professor at the University of Texas at Austin, Nobel laureate in chemistry, author of *The End of Certainty: Time, Chaos, and the New Laws of Nature*

Prince: musician, music producer, actor

Wolfgang Puck: chef, restaurateur, entrepreneur

Pussy Riot: Maria Alyokhina and Nadezhda Tolokonnikova, the two members of the Russian feminist punk rock group who served time in prison

Steven Quartz: philosopher, professor at California Institute of Technology, specializing in the brain's value systems and how they interact with culture

James Quinlivan: analyst at the RAND Corporation, specializing in introducing change and technology into large organizations

William C. Rader: psychiatrist, administers stem cell injections for a variety of illnesses

Jason Randal: magician, mentalist

Ronald Reagan: president of the United States, 1981–1989

Sumner Redstone: media magnate, businessman, chairman of CBS, chairman of Viacom

Judith Regan: editor, book publisher

Eddie Rehfeldt: executive creative director for the communications firm Waggener Edstrom

David Remnick: journalist, author, editor of the *New Yorker,* winner of the Pulitzer Prize

David Rhodes: president of CBS News, former vice president of news for Fox News

Matthieu Ricard: Buddhist monk, photographer, author of *Happiness: A Guide to Developing Life's Most Important Skill*

Condoleezza Rice: U.S. secretary of state, 2005–2009, former U.S. national security advisor, former provost at Stanford University, professor of political economy at the Stanford Graduate School of Business

Frank Rich: journalist, author, former columnist for the *New York Times,* editor at large for *New York* magazine

Michael Rinder: activist and former senior executive for the Church of Scientology International

Richard Riordan: mayor of Los Angeles, 1993–2001, businessman

Tony Robbins: life coach, author, motivational speaker

Robert Wilson and Richard Hutton: criminal defense attorneys

Brian L. Roberts: chairman and CEO of Comcast Corporation

Burton B. Roberts: chief administrative judge, New York Supreme Court in the Bronx, model for a character in Tom Wolfe's novel *The Bonfire of the Vanities*

Michael Roberts: fashion journalist, fashion and style director at *Vanity Fair,* former fashion director at the *New Yorker*

Joe Robinson: speaker and trainer on work-life balance and productivity

Gerry Roche: senior chairman of Heidrick & Struggles, a business executive recruiting firm

Aaron Rose: film director, art-show curator, writer

Charlie Rose: journalist, TV interviewer, host of PBS's *Charlie Rose*

Maer Roshan: writer, editor, entrepreneur who launched *Radar* magazine and radaronline.com

Pasquale Rotella: founder of Insomniac Events, which produces music festival Electric Daisy Carnival

Karl Rove: Republican political consultant, chief strategist for George W. Bush presidential campaign, senior advisor and deputy chief of staff during the George W. Bush administration

Rick Rubin: record producer, founder of Def Jam Records

Ed Ruscha: pop artist

Salman Rushdie: novelist, author of *Midnight's Children* and *The Satanic Verses,* winner of the Booker Prize

RZA: leader of Wu-Tang Clan, musician, actor, music producer

Charles Saatchi: cofounder of the advertising agency Saatchi & Saatchi, cofounder of the advertising agency M&C Saatchi

Jeffrey Sachs: economist, professor at Columbia University, director of the Earth Institute at Columbia University

Oliver Sacks: neurologist, author, professor at New York University School of Medicine

Carl Sagan: astronomer, astrophysicist, cosmologist, author, professor at Cornell University, narrated and cowrote the PBS TV series *Cosmos*

Jonas Salk: scientist, developer of the first polio vaccine, founder of the Salk Institute for Biological Studies

Jerry Saltz: art critic for *New York* magazine

James Sanders: scholar of the Old Testament and one of the editors of the Dead Sea Scrolls

Shawn Sanford: director of lifestyle marketing at Microsoft

Robert Sapolsky: neuroendocrinologist, professor at Stanford School of Medicine

John Sarno: professor of rehabilitation medicine at New York University School of Medicine

Michael Scheuer: former CIA intelligence officer, former chief of the Osama bin Laden tracking unit in the CIA's Counterterrorism Center, author

Paul Schimmel: former chief curator at the Museum of Contemporary Art, Los Angeles

Julian Schnabel: artist, filmmaker

Howard Schultz: chairman and CEO of Starbucks

John H. Schwarz: theoretical physicist, professor at California Institute of Technology, one of the fathers of string theory

David Scott: Apollo-era astronaut, first person to drive on the moon

Mary Lynn Scovazzo: orthopedic surgeon, specialist in sports medicine

Terrence Sejnowski: professor, directs the Computational Neurobiology Laboratory at the Salk Institute for Biological Studies

Marshall Sella: journalist for *GQ, New York* magazine, and the *New York Times Magazine*

Al Sharpton: Baptist minister, civil rights activist, talk-show host

Daniel Sheehan: constitutional and public interest lawyer, cofounder of the Christic Institute and founder of the Romero Institute

Mike Sheehan: New York City police officer who became a news reporter

Yoshio Shimomura: consultant on Japanese culture

Ronald K. Siegel: psychopharmacologist, author

Michael Sigman: former president and publisher of *LA Weekly*

Sanford Sigoloff: businessman, corporate turnaround expert

Ben Silbermann: entrepreneur, cofounder and CEO of Pinterest

Simon Sinek: former advertising executive, motivational speaker, author of *Start with Why: How Great Leaders Inspire Everyone to Take Action*

Mike Skinner: musician, music producer, leader of English hip-hop project the Streets

Slick Rick: musician, music producer

Anthony Slide: journalist, author, expert on the history of popular entertainment

Carlos Slim: Mexican businessman, investor, philanthropist

Gary Small: professor of psychiatry at UCLA Medical School, director of UCLA Center on Aging

Fred Smith: founder, chairman, and CEO of FedEx Corp.

Rick Smolan: cocreator of the Day in the Life book series, former photographer for *National Geographic*, *Time* and *Life* magazines

Frank Snepp: journalist, former CIA agent and analyst during the Vietnam War

Scott Snyder: comic book and short-story writer

Scott Andrew Snyder and Tracy Forman-Snyder: design and art direction, Arkitip

Johnny Spain: one of the "San Quentin Six," who attempted to escape from San Quentin State Prison in 1971

Gerry Spence: famed trial lawyer, never lost a criminal case as a prosecutor or a defense attorney

Art Spiegelman: cartoonist, illustrator, author of *Maus*, winner of the Pulitzer Prize

Eliot Spitzer: governor of New York, 2007–2008, former attorney general of New York

Peter Stan: analyst and economic theorist at RAND Corporation

Gwen Stefani: musician, fashion designer

Howard Stern: radio and TV personality

Cyndi Stivers: journalist, former editor in chief of *Time Out New York*

Biz Stone: cofounder of Twitter

Neil Strauss: author of *The Game: Penetrating the Secret Society of Pickup Artists*

Yancey Strickler: cofounder and CEO of Kickstarter

James Surowiecki: journalist, business and financial columnist for the *New Yorker*

Eric Sussman: senior lecturer at UCLA School of Management, president of Amber Capital

t.A.T.u.: Russian music duo

André Leon Talley: contributor and former editor at large for *Vogue*

Amy Tan: author of *The Joy Luck Club*

Gerald Tarlow: clinical psychologist and therapist

Ron Teeguarden: herbalist, explores Asian healing techniques

Edward Teller: theoretical physicist, father of the hydrogen bomb

Ed Templeton: professional skateboarder, founder of skateboard company Toy Machine

Margaret Thatcher: prime minister of the United Kingdom, 1979–1990

Lynn Tilton: investor, businesswoman, founder and CEO of Patriarch Partners

Justin Timberlake: musician, actor

Jeffrey Toobin: journalist, author, lawyer, staff writer for the *New Yorker*, senior legal analyst for CNN

Abdullah Toukan: CEO of Strategic Analysis and Global Risk Assessment (SAGRA) Center, Jordan

Robert Trivers: evolutionary biologist, professor at Rutgers University

Richard Turco: atmospheric scientist, professor emeritus at UCLA, MacArthur Fellowship recipient

Ted Turner: media mogul, founder of CNN

Richard Tyler: fashion designer

Tim Uyeki: epidemiologist at U.S. Centers for Disease Control and Prevention

Craig Venter: biochemist, geneticist, entrepreneur, one of the first to sequence the human genome

René-Thierry Magon de la Villehuchet: French aristocrat, money manager, one of the founders of Access International Advisors, which was caught in the Madoff investment scandal

Bill Viola: video artist whose work explores stages of consciousness

Jefferson Wagner: former Malibu councilman, owner of Zuma Jay Surfboards

Rufus Wainwright: musician

John Walsh: art historian, curator, former director of the J. Paul Getty Museum

Andy Warhol: Pop artist

Robert Watkins: businessman, chairman of the U.S. Rugby Foundation

Kenneth Watman: analyst at RAND Corporation specializing in strategic defense and nuclear deterrence

James Watson: molecular biologist, geneticist, zoologist, codiscoverer of the structure of DNA, Nobel laureate in medicine

Andrew Weil: physician, naturopath, teacher, writer on holistic health

Jann Wenner: cofounder and publisher of *Rolling Stone,* owner of *Men's Journal* and *US Weekly*

Kanye West: musician, music producer, fashion designer

Michael West: gerontologist, entrepreneur, stem cell researcher, works on regenerative medicine

Floyd Red Crow Westerman: musician, political activist for Native American causes

Vivienne Westwood: fashion designer who developed modern punk and new wave fashions

Peter Whybrow: psychiatrist, endocrinologist, researches hormones and manic-depression

Hugh Wilhere: spokesman for the Church of Scientology

Pharrell Williams: musician, music producer, fashion designer

Serena Williams: professional tennis player

Willie L. Williams: former police chief of Los Angeles

Marianne Williamson: spiritual teacher, New Age guru

Ian Wilmut: embryologist, led the team of researchers who first successfully cloned a mammal (a sheep named Dolly)

E. O. Wilson: biologist, author, professor emeritus at Harvard University, two-time winner of the Pulitzer Prize

Oprah Winfrey: founder and chairwoman of the Oprah Winfrey Network, actress, author

George C. Wolfe: playwright, theater director, two-time winner of the Tony Award

Steve Wozniak: cofounder of Apple Inc., designer of Apple I and Apple II computers, inventor

John D. Wren: president and CEO of marketing and communications company Omnicom

Will Wright: game designer, creator of Sim City and The Sims

Steve Wynn: businessman, Las Vegas casino magnate

Gideon Yago: writer, former correspondent for *MTV News*

Eitan Yardeni: teacher and spiritual counselor at the Kabbalah Centre

Daniel Yergin: economist, author of *The Prize: The Epic Quest for Oil, Money and Power*, winner of the Pulitzer Prize

Dan York: chief content officer at DirecTV, former president of content and advertising sales, AT&T

Michael W. Young: geneticist, professor at The Rockefeller University, specializing in the biological clock and circadian rhythms

Shinzen Young: meditation teacher

Eran Zaidel: neuropsychologist, professor at UCLA, expert in hemispheric interaction in the human brain

Howard Zinn: historian, political scientist, professor at Boston University, author of *A People's History of the United States*

Appendix: How to Have a Curiosity Conversation

We've talked throughout *A Curious Mind* about how to use questions, how to use curiosity, to make your daily life better. But maybe you want to try what I did: Maybe you want to have some curiosity conversations, to sit down with a few really interesting people and try to understand how they see the world differently than you do.

Curiosity conversations can help give you a bigger life. They can do for you what they have done for me—they can help you step out of your own world, they can widen your perspective, they can give you a taste of experiences you won't have on your own.

Starter Conversations

Everyone has their own style, but I'd recommend starting close to home. That's what I did, in fact. Think about your immediate circle of relatives, friends, acquaintances, work-related colleagues. Maybe there are a few people with intriguing jobs or very different experiences—of education, upbringing, culture, or people who work in your business but in a different arena.

That's a great place to start, a good place to get a feel for how a curiosity conversation works. Pick someone, and ask if they'll make a date to talk to you for twenty minutes or so— and specify what you want to talk about.

"I've always been curious about your work, I'm trying to broaden my sense of that world, and I was wondering if you'd be willing to spend twenty minutes talking to me about what you do, what the challenges and the satisfactions are."

Or . . .

"I've always been curious about how you ended up as [whatever their profession is], and I was wondering if you'd be willing to spend twenty minutes talking to me about what it took to get where you are—what the key turning points in your career have been."

Here are a few tips for when someone agrees to talk to you—whether they are a family member, an acquaintance, or a friend of a friend:

- Be clear that you want to hear their story. You're not looking for a job, you're not looking for advice about your own situation or any challenges you're facing. You're curious about them.
- Even if the person you're talking to is someone you know well, be respectful—treat the occasion with just a tinge of formality, because you want to talk about things you don't

normally; dress well; be on time; be appreciative of their time even as you sit down to begin.

- Think in advance about what you'd most hope to get out of the conversation, and think of a handful of open-ended questions that will get the person talking about what you're most interested in: "What was your first professional success?" "Why did you decide to do [whatever their job is]?" "Tell me about a couple of big challenges you had to overcome." "What has been your biggest surprise?" "How did you end up living in [their city]?" "What's the part of what you do that outsiders don't appreciate?"

- Don't be a slave to your prepared questions. Be just the opposite: Listen closely, and be a good conversationalist. Pick up on what the person you're talking to is saying, and ask questions that expand on the stories they tell or the points they make.

- Don't share your own story or your own observations. Listen. Ask questions. The goal is for you to learn as much about the person you're talking to as you can in the time you have. If you're talking, you're not learning about the other person.

- Be respectful of the person's time, without unnecessarily cutting off a great conversation. If they agree to give you twenty minutes, keep track of the time. Even if things are going well, when the allotted time has passed, it's okay to say something like, "I don't want to take too much of your time and it's been twenty minutes" or "It's been twenty minutes, perhaps I should let you go." People will often say, "I'm enjoying this, I can give you a few more minutes."

- Be grateful. Don't just say thank you, give the best compliment for a conversation like this: "That was so interesting." And send a very brief follow-up email thank you, perhaps highlighting one story or point they made that you particularly enjoyed, or that was particularly eye-opening for you. That thank-you email shouldn't ask for anything more—it should be written so the person who gave you his or her time doesn't even need to reply.

Curiosity Conversations Farther Afield

Conversations with people outside your own circle or with strangers are harder to arrange, but they can be fascinating, even thrilling.

Who should you approach? Think about your own interests—whether it's college football or astrophysics or cooking, your community almost surely has local experts. When you read the paper or watch the local news, pay attention to people who make an impression on you. Search out experts at your local university.

Setting up curiosity conversations with people outside your own circle requires a little more planning and discretion:

- First, once you've identified someone you'd like to sit and talk to for twenty minutes, consider whether you might know someone who knows that person. Get in touch with the person you know, explain who you want to talk to, and ask if you can use your acquaintance's name. An email that begins, "I'm writing at the suggestion of [name of mutual acquaintance]," establishes immediate credibility.

- If you are trying to meet someone who is totally outside of your circle, use your own credentials and strong interest up front. "I'm a vice president at the local hospital, and I have a lifelong interest in astronomy. I was wondering if you'd be willing to spend twenty minutes talking to me about your own work and the current state of the field. I appreciate that you don't know me, but I'm writing out of genuine curiosity—I don't want anything more than a twenty-minute conversation, at your convenience."

- You may hear back from an assistant asking for a little more information—and some people may find the request a little unusual. Explain what you're hoping for. Be clear that you're not seeking a job, or advice, or a career change—you are simply trying to understand a little about someone with real achievements in a field you care about.

- If you get an appointment, make sure to do as much reading as possible about the person you're going to see, as well as their field. That can help you ask good questions about their career track or their avocations. But it's a fine line: be respectful of people's privacy.

- Pay attention not just to what the person you're talking to says, but how they say it. Often there is as much information in people's tone, in the way they tell a story or respond to a question, as in the answer itself.
- The tips about starter conversations apply—along with your own experience of having those starter conversations. Have questions in advance, but let the conversation flow based on what you learn; make your side of the conversation questions—not your own thoughts; be respectful of the clock; be grateful in person and in a very brief follow-up email. If an assistant helps set up a curiosity conversation, be sure to include that person in your thank-you note.

Curiosity Takeaways

What you'll discover is that people love talking about themselves—about their work, about their challenges, about the story of how they arrived where they are.

The hardest part is the very beginning.

In a formal curiosity conversation, I would recommend not taking notes—the goal is a good conversation. Taking notes might just make someone uncomfortable.

But when you've left a person's office, it's valuable to spend just a few minutes thinking about what the most surprising thing you learned was; what the person's tone and personality was like, compared to what you might have imagined; what choices they've made that were different than you might have made in the same circumstances.

And you don't need to have curiosity conversations in formal settings that you set up. You meet people all the time. The person next to you on the airplane or at the wedding quite likely has a fascinating story and comes from a world different from yours—and all you have to do in that setting is turn, smile, and introduce yourself to start a conversation. "Hi, I'm Brian, I work in the movie business—what do you do?"

Remember that if you're trying to learn something, you should be asking questions and listening to the answers rather than talking about yourself.

Curiosity Conversation 2.0: The Curiosity Dinner Party

You can take the principles above and extend them into a group atmosphere by hosting a gathering. Think of two or three interesting friends or acquaintances—they can be people who know one another or do not—preferably from different lines of work and different backgrounds.

Invite those people, and ask each of them to invite two or three of their most interesting friends or acquaintances. The result will be a group of selected people who are interconnected but (hopefully) very different from one another.

The dinner party can be as formal or informal as you like, but it should be in a place that is conducive to mingling. Use the suggestions above to kick off the dinner conversation and encourage each person to follow their own curiosity, ask questions, listen, and learn about one another.

Acknowledgments

Brian Grazer

The journalist Charlie Rose was the first person to seriously suggest a book about curiosity. He'd had me on his PBS interview show to talk about curiosity, and afterward he said, "You should do a book about this."

That was ten years ago. Charlie Rose planted the seed. Ron Howard—who knew about the incredible range of the curiosity conversations—would also occasionally nudge me to write a book. He feels like there is so much fun and insight packed into those decades of talking to people.

But I was always a little uncomfortable with the idea—a book about my curiosity seemed like it would be egotistical, and not that interesting to anyone else.

One afternoon in 2012 I was talking about the curiosity conversations with Bryan Lourd, one of my show business agents, and he said, "Why don't you write a book about that? Why don't you write a book about curiosity?" Richard Lovett,

Bryan's colleague at CAA, had suggested the same thing. I said that it didn't seem like a very interesting book. Bryan said, "No, not a book about *your* curiosity, a book about the journey curiosity has taken you on. A book about *curiosity*—not as some kind of accomplishment, but as something you use to explore the world."

That reframing of the idea—a book not about my curiosity, but about what curiosity has enabled me to do, about what curiosity can enable anyone to do—snapped the idea into focus for me.

I didn't want to write a book about all the people I'd had conversations with—I wanted to write about the impulse to have those conversations. I wanted to use the conversations to tell a story: the story of my steady discovery of the power of curiosity in my own life.

In the book, I tell the story of my grandmother, Sonia Schwartz, inspiring and nurturing my curiosity as a boy. There have been some similarly critical people who have supported my curious style as an adult.

The first among those is, in fact, Ron Howard, my closest professional colleague going back thirty years, my business partner at Imagine Entertainment, and my best friend. Ron is my sounding board, my supporter, my conscience, and he never stops encouraging my curiosity.

Michael Rosenberg has been helping Ron and me make movies in a businesslike fashion for twenty-six years. We often have fifteen or twenty projects going at once, and I am sure

Michael wasn't thinking I needed to add a book—requiring hours a week of time—to all our other demands. But he has been an enthusiastic supporter of the book from the start, and he has figured out how to gracefully add *A Curious Mind* to everything else we're doing. We would be lost without Michael's loyalty, determination, and quiet leadership.

Karen Kehela Sherwood was the first person to help me set up the "curiosity conversations," taking on a task I had done for years by myself. She brought the same determination to getting people to come and talk as I did, but she dramatically widened our range. She brought professionalism to the curiosity conversations, and she made my priorities her priorities—both things for which I am eternally grateful.

After Karen, many executives and assistants helped me continue the conversations over many years.

In 2006, Brad Grossman formalized the curiosity conversation process. He gave the curiosity conversations depth and structure, and he brought such honest interest in new people and new subjects that with his help I met people I never would have met on my own.

At Imagine, the help and guidance of many people has been indispensable, including Erica Huggins, Kim Roth, Robin Ruse-Rinehart Barris, Anna Culp, and Sage Shah. Hillary Messenger and Lee Dreyfuss get me through the day every day.

I want to thank my siblings, Nora and Gavin. They've been listening to my questions longer than anyone else. They keep me cheerfully connected to the real world, and the world in which we all grew up.

My kids are the joy of my life. Riley, Sage, Thomas, and Patrick are the best curiosity guides I've ever had—they each pull me into universes I would never get to visit without them.

My fiancée, Veronica Smiley, has been at my side throughout the creation of *A Curious Mind*, and she has been indispensable. Veronica sees the best in people, and she knows instinctively how to get the best out of me. Her generosity, her cheerfulness, and her sense of adventure are contagious.

In terms of getting curiosity from the idea for a book to the printed page, I am indebted to Simon Green at CAA for his work in getting the book published.

Jonathan Karp, the president and publisher of Simon & Schuster, understood the kind of book I wanted this to be from the beginning—and from the spark of the idea through the writing process, he has given us support and brilliant editing, and he has held on to a clear vision of the book and its possibilities, which have kept me focused.

Also at Simon & Schuster, Sydney Tanigawa gave *A Curious Mind* a careful and thoughtful word edit; the book is much better for her attention. We've had great support throughout Simon & Schuster: Megan Hogan, in Jonathan Karp's office; Cary Goldstein and Kellyn Patterson in publicity; Richard Rhorer and Dana Trocker in marketing; Irene Kheradi, Gina DiMascia, and Ffej Caplan in managing editorial; Jackie Seow, Christopher Lin, and Joy O'Meara in art and design; and Lisa

Erwin and Carla Benton in production and copyediting, as well as Judith Hancock for creating the book's index.

Finally, I want to thank my coauthor and collaborator, Charles Fishman, a nationally renowned journalist. He asks questions for a living, and he asked questions about curiosity that had never occurred to me. I know how much work goes into a movie or a TV show, but I had no idea how much work goes into a book. Charles has done a remarkable job shaping our own curiosity conversations into a completely original narrative. I often start our calls with the greeting "The Mighty Fish!" He has been exactly that.

Charles Fishman

I first heard about Brian Grazer's book project when my agent, Raphael Sagalyn, called and said, "I'm going to say a single word to you. Let's see if this one word is a book idea you might be interested in. The word is 'curiosity.'"

He had me immediately. There aren't many single-word topics as engaging and important as curiosity. And then Rafe told me the author was the Academy Award–winning producer Brian Grazer.

I want to thank Brian for the chance to step into his world and to think about curiosity in ways I had never considered. Brian is a master storyteller, and it has been fascinating, fun, and illuminating to work with him day after day bringing curiosity to life. His core belief in the power of curiosity to make everyone's life better is an inspiration.

I also want to thank Jonathan Karp for thinking this might be a project I'd be interested in. His support from the earliest conversations about how to shape the book until the final editing has been indispensable. Sydney Tanigawa, our editor at Simon & Schuster, has been patient and insightful.

The book would not have been written without the team at Imagine Entertainment. No one there ever hesitated to help or refused a single request. Thanks to Ron Howard, Michael Rosenberg, Erica Huggins, Kim Roth, Robin Ruse-Rinehart Barris, Anna Culp, and Sage Shah. Hillary Messenger and Lee Dreyfuss made sure I stayed connected to Brian. Their good humor never failed.

No book gets finished without the counsel of Rafe, the guidance of Geoff, or the patience and support of Trish, Nicolas, and Maya. My best curiosity conversations start and end with them.

Notes

Introduction: A Curious Mind and a Curious Book

1. Letter from Albert Einstein to his biographer Carl Seelig, March 11, 1952, cited in Alice Calaprice, ed., *The Expanded Quotable Einstein* (Princeton, NJ: Princeton University Press, 2000).

Chapter 1: There Is No Cure for Curiosity

1. This quote—perhaps the most razor-sharp take on curiosity's power—is widely attributed to the writer and poet Dorothy Parker, but no scholarly or online source has a citation for when Parker might have written or said it. The quote is also occasionally attributed to someone named Ellen Parr, but also without attribution, or any identifying information about Parr. The pair of lines do have the particular interlocking snap that is characteristic of Parker's turn of phrase.

2. For those younger than thirty, phone companies used to offer a remarkable service. If you needed a phone number, you simply dialed 4-1-1 on your telephone and an operator would look it up for you. The address too.

3. Forty years later, that is still the main phone number at Warner Bros., although now you also have to dial the area code: (818) 954-6000.

4. What kind of character was Sue Mengers? Pretty big, pretty fearsome. The 2013 Broadway play about Mengers's life was called *I'll Eat You Last.*

5. Google reports that the average number of searches per day in 2013 was

5,922,000,000. That's 4,112,500 each minute. www.statisticbrain.com /google-searches/, accessed October 10, 2014.

6. In the CBS TV series *Dallas*, the question of "Who shot J.R.?" became one of the most effective cliffhangers in modern storytelling—a masterful campaign in creating curiosity. The actor Larry Hagman, who played J.R. Ewing in the TV show, was shot in the concluding episode of the 1979–80 season, which aired March 21, 1980. The character who shot him was not revealed until an episode broadcast eight months later, on November 21, 1980.

Marketing—and curiosity—around the cliffhanger was so widespread that bookies laid odds and took bets on who the shooter would turn out to be, and "Who shot J.R.?" jokes even crept into the 1980 presidential campaign between Jimmy Carter and Ronald Reagan. The Republican campaign produced buttons reading, "The Democrats shot J.R."; President Carter joked that he would have no trouble with fund-raising if he could find out who had shot J.R.

CBS filmed five scenes, each with a different character shooting J.R. On the November 21 episode, the shooter was revealed to be Kristen Shepard, J.R.'s mistress (content.time.com/time/magazine/article/0,9171, 924376,00.html#paid-wall, accessed October 10, 2014).

If you're curious, the largest Powerball jackpot—the jackpot from the forty-five-state lottery in the U.S.—was $590.5 million, won on May 18, 2013, by a single-ticket holder, Gloria C. MacKenzie, eighty-four, with a ticket purchased at a Publix supermarket in Zephyrhills, Florida (www.npr .org/blogs/thetwo-way/2013/06/05/189018342/84-year-old-woman -claims-powerball-jackpot, accessed October 10, 2014).

7. Adults tend not to know the answer to "Why is the sky blue?" because although it's a simple question, and a simple experience, the answer itself is complicated. The sky is blue because of how light itself is made up.

Blue wavelengths of light are more easily scattered by the particles in the air than other colors, and so as sunlight streams from the sun to the ground, the blue light passing through the atmosphere gets scattered around, and we see that scattering as the sky being blue.

The blue color fades as you get higher up in the atmosphere. In a passenger jet, flying at six miles up (32,000 feet), the blue is already a little watery and thin. If you look up as you fly higher, the sky starts to look black—the black of space.

And the sky doesn't look blue when there is no light shining through it, of course. The blue goes away when the sun sets.

8. Genesis, 2:16–17. The citation is from the New International Version of the Bible, www.biblegateway.com, accessed October 18, 2014.

9. Genesis, 3:4–5. NIV.

10. Genesis, 3:6. NIV.

11. Genesis, 3:7. NIV.

12. It's an astonishing output by a studio, in terms of lasting cultural impact and quality in a short time. The movies by year:

A Clockwork Orange, 1971 (four Academy Award nominations)

Dirty Harry, 1971

Deliverance, 1972 (three Academy Award nominations)

The Exorcist, 1973 (two Academy Awards, ten nominations)

Blazing Saddles, 1974 (three Academy Award nominations)

The Towering Inferno, 1974 (three Academy Awards, eight nominations)

Dog Day Afternoon, 1975 (one Academy Award, six nominations)

All the President's Men, 1976 (four Academy Awards, eight nominations)

13. "A Strong Debut Helps, As a New Chief Tackles Sony's Movie Problems," Geraldine Fabrikant, *New York Times*, May 26, 1997.

14. When John Calley died in 2011, the *Los Angeles Times* used a picture of him sitting on a couch, one foot propped up on a coffee table (www.latimes .com/entertainment/news/movies/la-me-2011notables-calley,0,403960 .photo#axzz2qUMEKSCu, accessed October 10, 2014).

15. My office at Imagine Entertainment does have a desk, but I don't sit there very often. I have two couches, and that's where I work, notes spread out on the couch cushions or the coffee table, a console phone sitting on the cushion next to me.

16. Stop and think about yourself for a minute. Regardless of what work you

do—whether you work in movies or software, insurance or health care or advertising—imagine if you decided today that for the next six months you would meet a new person *every single day* in your industry. Not to have an hour-long conversation, just to meet them and talk for five minutes. Six months from now, you'd know one hundred fifty people in your own line of work you don't know right now. If even 10 percent of those people had something to offer—insight, connections, support for a project—that's fifteen new allies.

17. The piece ran in the *New Yorker*'s "Talk of the Town" section: "Want Ad: Beautiful Minds," by Lizzie Widdicombe, March 20, 2008.

18. According to the *Forbes* magazine list of the richest people in the world, Carlos Slim was number one when I met him, and as of the end of 2014, he was also number one. But the top three—Slim, Microsoft founder Bill Gates, and investor Warren Buffett—shift around depending on the movement of the stock market.

Chapter 2: The Police Chief, the Movie Mogul, and the Father of the H-Bomb: Thinking Like Other People

1. The full line from Vladimir Nabokov is: "Curiosity in its turn is insubordination in its purest form." It comes from the 1947 novel *Bend Sinister* (New York: Vintage Classic Paperback, 2012), 46.

2. President Bush used the speech to denounce the rioting, which he said "is not about civil rights" and "not a message of protest" but "the brutality of a mob, pure and simple." But he also said of the beating of Rodney King: "What you saw and what I saw on the TV video was revolting. I felt anger. I felt pain. How can I explain this to my grandchildren?" The text of Bush's May 1, 1992, speech is here: www.presidency.ucsb.edu/ws/?pid=20910, accessed October 10, 2014.

3. In the wake of the Rodney King beating—before the officers were tried—there was an investigative commission into the practices of the Los Angeles Police Department, and into Gates's leadership, and Gates announced in the summer of 1991 that he would resign. He then postponed his retire-

ment several times—and even threatened to postpone leaving after his successor, Willie Williams, the chief in Philadelphia, was hired.

Here are several accounts of Gates's reluctant departure:

Robert Reinhold, "Head of Police in Philadelphia Chosen for Chief in Los Angeles," *New York Times*, April 16, 1992, www.nytimes.com/1992/04 /16/us/head-of-police-in-philadelphia-chosen-for-chief-in-los-angeles .html, accessed October 10, 2014.

Richard A. Serrano and James Rainey, "Gates Says He Bluffed Staying, Lashes Critics," *Los Angeles Times*, June 9, 1992, articles.latimes.com /1992-06-09/news/mn-188_1_police-department, accessed October 10, 2014.

Richard A. Serrano, "Williams Takes Oath as New Police Chief," *Los Angeles Times*, June 27, 1992, articles.latimes.com/1992-06-27/news/ mn-828_1_police-commission, accessed October 10, 2014.

4. Daryl Gates was a protégé of William H. Parker, the man for whom the old LAPD headquarters, Parker Center, was named. Early in his career, as a young patrol officer, Gates was assigned to be Chief Parker's driver, a job in which Gates got to see up close the everyday acquisition and use of authority. Later, Gates was Parker's executive officer. Parker was the longest-serving LAPD chief, at sixteen years (1950 to 1966); Gates is the second-longest-serving chief, at fourteen years.

5. Novelists and painters can rework the same topics, characters, and themes over and over again—many popular book series involve the same characters in very similar plots. Actors, directors, and others in Hollywood are supposed to avoid doing that, for fear of being typecast, or "falling into a rut."

6. I talked to Michael Scheuer just after he left the CIA in 2004, when his book *Imperial Hubris,* about being a front-line operative, came out. For an account of Scheuer's increasingly extreme views since then, read David Frum, in the *Daily Beast,* January 3, 2014: "Michael Scheuer's Meltdown," www.thedailybeast.com/articles/2014/01/03/michael-scheuer-s-meltdown.html, accessed October 10, 2014.

7. This list comes from the *New York Times* obituary of Lew Wasserman, who died June 3, 2002. "Lew Wasserman, 89, is Dead; Last of Hollywood's Moguls," by Jonathan Kandell, *New York Times*, June 4, 2002. http://www.nytimes.com/2002/06/04/business/lew-wasserman-89-is-dead-last-of-hollywood-s-moguls.html, accessed October 10, 2014.

8. People have been trying to eat and drink in cars since roads were smoothed out, but the search for a way of securing drinks inside cars really took off during the 1950s, with the invention of the drive-in hamburger stand. For a brief, charming history of the cup holder, see Sam Dean, "The History of the Car Cup Holder," *Bon Appétit*, February 18, 2013, www.bonappetit.com/trends/article/the-history-of-the-car-cup-holder, accessed October 10, 2014.

9. "Turning an Icon on Its Head," *Chief Executive*, July 2003, chiefexecutive.net/turning-an-icon-on-its-head, accessed October 10, 2014. The story of Paul Brown imagining himself as liquid silicone is found in this second account of the invention of the upside-down bottle—the valve was first used in shampoo bottles: Frank Greve, "Ketchup Squeezes Competition with Upside-Down, Bigger Bottle," McClatchey Newspapers, June 25, 2007, www.mcclatchydc.com/2007/06/28/17335/ketchup-is-better-with-upside.html, accessed October 10, 2014.

10. Bruce Brown and Scott D. Anthony, "How P&G Tripled Its Innovation Success Rate," *Harvard Business Review*, June 2011 (PDF file), www.hbsclubwdc.net/images.html?file_id=xtypsHwtheU%3D, accessed October 10, 2014.

11. Sam Walton tells the story of creating Wal-Mart, and refining his business practices and his curiosity, in his autobiography, *Made in America* (New York: Bantam Books, 1993, with John Huey). Walton's curiosity was legendary. One fellow retail executive recalls meeting Walton and said, "He proceed[ed] to extract every piece of information in your possession" (p. 105).

The word "curiosity" appears twice in Walton's 346-page book, most notably in a quote from Sam Walton's wife, Helen, describing her distaste at having become a public figure: "What I hate is being the object of curiosity. People are so curious about everything, and so we are just public conversation. The whole thing just makes me mad when I think about it. I mean, I hate it" (p. 98). The other use of curiosity is Walton's surprise at being welcomed in the headquarters of his retail competitors early on, while he was trying to learn how other people ran their stores. "As often as not, they'd let me in, maybe out of curiosity" (p. 104). Walton, too, didn't use the word to credit his own curiosity.

12. The frequency of the words "creativity," "innovation," and "curiosity" in the U.S. media comes from Nexis database searches of the category "US Newspapers and Wires" starting January 1, 1980. As the words appeared more and more frequently, the Nexis searches were done week by week for January and June of each year, to get representative counts.

Chapter 3: The Curiosity Inside the Story

1. Jonathan Gottschall, *The Storytelling Animal* (New York: Houghton Mifflin, 2012), 3.

2. You can Google the phrase "billion-dollar film franchises," and you get a list from the folks at Nash Information Services, who produce movie-industry news and data focused on the financial performance of movies in a publication called *The Numbers*. Nash's list of movie "franchises" shows that at the U.S. box office, fourteen series of U.S. movies have made $1 billion or more. If you include international sales, the numbers are much larger. In all, forty-seven movie series have grossed more than $1 billion in box office sales. The up-to-date list is here: www.the-numbers.com/movies /franchises/, accessed October 18, 2014. Nash's *The Numbers* website also says that the movies I have produced in the last thirty-five years have gross sales of $5,647,276,060. Details here: www.the-numbers.com/person /208890401-Brian-Grazer#tab=summary, accessed October 18, 2014.

3. What parts of the movie *Apollo 13* take liberties with what actually happened? If you're curious, here are a handful of websites that answer the question, including a long interview with T. K. Mattingly, the astronaut

who was bumped from the flight at the last minute because he was exposed to German measles:

Ken Mattingly on the movie *Apollo 13*: www.universetoday.com /101531/ken-mattingly-explains-how-the-apollo-13-movie-differed -from-real-life/, accessed October 18, 2014.

From the official NASA oral history website: www.jsc.nasa.gov/history /oral_histories/MattinglyTK/MattinglyTK_11-6-01.htm, accessed October 18, 2014.

From Space.com, "Apollo 13: Facts About NASA's Near Disaster": www.space.com/17250-apollo-13-facts.html, accessed October 18, 2014.

4. "How Biblically Accurate is *Noah*?" Miriam Krule, *Slate*, March 28, 2014, www.slate.com/blogs/browbeat/2014/03/28/noah_movie_biblical _accuracy_how_the_darren_aronofsky_movie_departs_from.html, accessed October 18, 2014.

5. How did NPR discover its listeners were having "driveway moments"? A former senior news executive for NPR told me the network receives letters (and now emails) from listeners saying they did not go into the house when they got home—they sat in their cars until the story to which they were listening was over.

6. If you're not a regular listener to National Public Radio, and don't know what it feels like to be so bewitched by a radio story that you can't leave your car, here's a collection of dozens of NPR stories that are considered "driveway moments." Listen to one or two. You'll see: www.npr.org/series /700000/driveway-moments, accessed October 18, 2014.

Chapter 4: **Curiosity as a Superhero Power**

1. James Stephens (1880–1950) was a popular Irish poet and novelist in the early twentieth century. This line is from *The Crock of Gold* (London: Macmillan, 1912), 9 (viewable via books.google.com).

The full sentence, discussed later in the chapter, is: "Curiosity will conquer fear even more than bravery will; indeed, it has led many people into dangers which mere physical courage would shudder away from, for hunger and love and curiosity are the great impelling forces of life."

Stephens's death merited a seven-paragraph obituary in the *New York Times*: query.nytimes.com/mem/archive-free/pdf?res=9905E3DC103EEF 3BBC4F51DFB467838B649EDE, accessed October 18, 2014.

2. Isaac Asmiov's productivity as an author was so impressive that the *New York Times* obituary of him details the number of books he wrote decade by decade—in the obituary's fourth paragraph. Mervyn Rothstein, "Isaac Asimov, Whose Thoughts and Books Traveled the Universe, Is Dead at 72," *New York Times*, April 7, 1992, www.nytimes.com/books/97/03/23 /lifetimes/asi-v-obit.html, accessed October 18, 2014.

There is a catalog of every book Asimov wrote online, compiled by Ed Seiler, with the apparent assistance of Asimov: www.asimovonline.com /oldsite/asimov_catalogue.html, accessed October 18, 2014.

3. In reconstructing this meeting, we exchanged emails with Janet Jeppson Asimov about my brief visit twenty-eight years ago. She has no memory of it, and she apologized for any rudeness. She also said that, although it wasn't publicly known at the time, Isaac Asimov was already infected with the HIV virus that would kill him six years later, and he was already often ill. Janet Asimov said her impatience may well have been a result of— entirely understandable—protectiveness of her husband.

4. The *New York Times* story of the prostitution ring run out of New York's morgue is just as fun as I remember it—and is practically the outline for a movie script. It ran on August 28, 1976, opposite the obituaries in the "Metro" section. The opening sentence reports that the men running the call-girl ring often "chauffer[ed] prostitutes to clients in the Medical Examiner's official car." The *Times* never did report what became of the charges against those men—nor did any other media outlet. Here is the original story (PDF): query.nytimes.com/mem/archive/pdf?res=F20617FC 3B5E16738DDDA10A94D0405B868BF1D3, accessed October 18, 2014.

5. The movie executive and journalist Beverly Gray gives a detailed account of the creation of *Night Shift* and *Splash* in her biography of Ron Howard,

Ron Howard: From Mayberry to the Moon . . . and Beyond (Nashville, TN: Rutledge Hill Press, 2003).

6. *Newsweek* did a story on the selling of the rights to *How the Grinch Stole Christmas!*: "The Grinch's Gatekeeper," November 12, 2000, www.news week.com/grinchs-gatekeeper-156985, accessed October 18, 2014.

Audrey's "GRINCH" license plate was noted in an Associated Press profile from 2004, the year that Theodor Geisel would have turned 100: "A Seussian Pair of Shoulders," by Michelle Morgante, Associated Press, February 28, 2004, published in the *Los Angeles Times*, articles.latimes.com /2004/feb/28/entertainment/et-morgante28, accessed October 18, 2014.

That Dr. Seuss had used the "GRINCH" license plate is noted in Charles Cohen's biography of him: *The Seuss, the Whole Seuss, and Nothing but the Seuss: A Visual Biography of Theodore Seuss Geisel* (New York: Random House, 2004), 330.

7. *Dr. Seuss' How the Grinch Stole Christmas!* was a huge hit in the Christmas movie season in 2000. It spent four weeks as the number-one movie in the country, and although it only debuted on November 17, it was the highest grossing movie of 2000 (ultimately making about $345 million), and is the second-highest-grossing movie of the Christmas season ever, after *Home Alone*. *Grinch* was nominated for three Academy Awards—for costume design, makeup, and art direction/set direction—and won for makeup.

8. Sales figures for Theodor Geisel's books in 2013 come from *Publisher's Weekly*: Diane Roback, "For Children's Books in 2013, Divergent Led the Pack," March 14, 2014, www.publishersweekly.com/pw/by-topic/childrens /childrens-industry-news/article/61447-for-children-s-books-in-2013 -divergent-led-the-pack-facts-figures-2013.html, accessed October 18, 2014.

The *New York Times* reported Seuss's total sales at 600 million copies on the seventy-fifth anniversary of the publication of *And to Think That I Saw It on Mulberry Street*: Michael Winerip, "Mulberry Street May Fade, But 'Mulberry Street' Shines On," January 29, 2012, www.nytimes.com/2012 /01/30/education/dr-seuss-book-mulberry-street-turns-75.html, accessed October 18, 2014.

The story of Geisel being rejected twenty-seven times before his first book was published is often repeated, but the details are worth relating. Geisel says he was walking home, stinging from the book's twenty-seventh rejection, with the manuscript and drawings for *Mulberry Street* under his arm, when an acquaintance from his student days at Dartmouth College bumped into him on the sidewalk on Madison Avenue in New York City. Mike McClintock asked what Geisel was carrying. "That's a book no one will publish," said Geisel. "I'm lugging it home to burn." McClintock had just that morning been made editor of children's books at Vanguard; he invited Geisel up to his office, and McClintock and his publisher bought *Mulberry Street* that day. When the book came out, the legendary book reviewer for the *New Yorker*, Clifton Fadiman, captured it in a single sentence: "They say it's for children, but better get a copy for yourself and marvel at the good Dr. Seuss's impossible pictures and the moral tale of the little boy who exaggerated not wisely but too well." Geisel would later say of meeting McClintock on the street, "[I]f I'd been going down the other side of Madison Avenue, I'd be in the dry-cleaning business today."

The story of Geisel meeting McClintock on Madison Avenue is well told in: Judith Morgan and Neil Morgan, *Dr. Seuss & Mr. Geisel: A Biography* (New York: Da Capo Press, 1995), 81–82. The Fadiman review, cited pp. 83–84.

9. James Reginato, "The mogul: Brian Grazer, whose movies have grossed $10.5 billion, is arguably the most successful producer in town—and surely the most recognizable. Is it the hair?" *W* magazine, February 1, 2004.

10. The *New York Post* did a brief story on the Cuba trip: "Castro Butters Up Media Moguls," February 15, 2001, 10.

Chapter 5: **Every Conversation Is a Curiosity Conversation**

1. Brené Brown is a research professor at the University of Houston Graduate College of Social Work. Her research focuses on shame and vulnerability, and she is the author of several best-selling books. She calls herself

"a researcher and a storyteller," and often says, "Maybe stories are just data with a soul." Her talk at TEDxHouston in June 2010—"The Power of Vulnerability"—is the fourth-most-watched TED talk ever, at 17 million views as of the end of 2014: www.ted.com/talks/brene_brown_on _vulnerability, accessed October 18, 2014.

2. Bianca Bosker, "Google Design: Why Google.com Homepage Looks So Simple," *Huffington Post*, March 27, 2012, www.huffingtonpost.com/2012 /03/27/google-design-sergey-brin_n_1384074.html, accessed October 18, 2014.

3. From the website poliotoday.org. The history section is here, with cultural impact and statistics: poliotoday.org/?page_id=13, accessed October 18, 2014.

   The website poliotoday.org is created and maintained by Jonas Salk's research organization, the Salk Institute for Biological Studies.

4. This list of polio survivors comes from the compilation on Wikipedia, which contains source citations for each person listed: en.wikipedia.org /wiki/List_of_poliomyelitis_survivors, accessed October 18, 2014.

5. One account of the often-controversial development of the polio vaccine is here: www.chemheritage.org/discover/online-resources/chemistry-in-history /themes/pharmaceuticals/preventing-and-treating-infectious-diseases /salk-and-sabin.aspx, accessed October 18, 2014.

6. Harold M. Schmeck, Jr., "Dr. Jonas Salk, Whose Vaccine Turned Tide on Polio, Dies at 80," *New York Times*, June 24, 1995, www.nytimes.com/1995 /06/24/obituaries/dr-jonas-salk-whose-vaccine-turned-tide-on-polio -dies-at-80.html, accessed October 18, 2014.

Chapter 6: **Good Taste and the Power of Anti-Curiosity**

1. Carl Sagan said this in a TV interview with Charlie Rose, May, 27, 1996, *The Charlie Rose Show*, PBS. The full interview is available on YouTube: www.youtube.com/watch?v=U8HEwO-2L4w, accessed October 18, 2014.

   At the time of the interview, astronomer and author Sagan was ill with bone marrow cancer. He died six months later, on December 20, 1996.

2. Denzel Washington said he would only do *American Gangster* if, in the end, the character he was playing, heroin dealer Frank Lucas, got punished.

3. The ticker trading symbol for Imagine on the NASDAQ was IFEI— Imagine Films Entertainment Inc.

Chapter 7: The Golden Age of Curiosity

1. From Arthur C. Clarke's 1951 book predicting the future of space travel: *The Exploration of Space* (New York: Harper and Brothers, 1951, since re-issued), chapter 18, p. 187.

2. Bees are surprisingly fast: they cruise along at about fifteen miles an hour and can go twenty miles an hour when they need to. So they are as fast as a slow-moving car—but up close, given their small size, they seem to be going quite fast.

    More on the speed of flying bees at this site from the University of California: ucanr.edu/blogs/blogcore/postdetail.cfm?postnum=10898, accessed October 18, 2014.

3. An excellent scientific biography of Robert Hooke: Michael W. Davidson, "Robert Hooke: Physics, Architecture, Astronomy, Paleontology, Biology," *LabMedicine* 41, 180–82.

    Available online: labmed.ascpjournals.org/content/41/3/180.full, accessed October 18, 2014.

4. Curiosity as "an outlaw impulse," from Barbara M. Benedict, *Curiosity: A Cultural History of Early Modern Inquiry* (Chicago: University of Chicago Press, 2001), 25.

5. Beina Xu, "Media Censorship in China," *Council on Foreign Relations*, February 12, 2014, www.cfr.org/china/media-censorship-china/p11515, accessed October 18, 2014.

6. The Karl Marx quote is often miscited as, "Religion is the opiate of the masses." The full context of the quote is revealing, because Marx was making an observation on the oppression and misery of the working class, which he thought religion tried to both paper over and justify. The full quote, which comes from Marx' *Critique of the Hegelian Philosophy of Right*

(Cambridge University Press, 1977, p. 131), is: "The wretchedness of religion is at once an expression of and a protest against real wretchedness. Religion is the sigh of the oppressed creature, the heart of a heartless world and the soul of soulless conditions. It is the opium of the people.

"The abolition of religion as the illusory happiness of the people is a demand for their true happiness. The call to abandon illusions about their condition is the call to abandon a condition which requires illusions. Thus, the critique of religion is the critique in embryo of the vale of tears of which religion is the halo."

Index

Academy Award–winning producer Brian Grazer has been making movies and television programs for more than thirty years. As both a writer and producer, he has personally been nominated for four Academy Awards. In 2002 he won the Best Picture Oscar for *A Beautiful Mind*.

In addition to *A Beautiful Mind*, Grazer's films include *Apollo 13*, *Friday Night Lights*, *American Gangster*, *8 Mile*, *Frost/Nixon*, *Liar Liar*, and *Splash*. The TV series Grazer has produced include *24*, *Arrested Development*, *Parenthood*, *Sports Night*, *Empire*, and *Friday Night Lights*.

Over the years, Grazer's films and TV shows have been nominated for a total of forty-three Oscars and 149 Emmys. His movies have generated more than $13 billion in worldwide theatrical, music, and video grosses. Reflecting this combination of commercial and artistic achievement, the Producers Guild of America honored Grazer with the David O. Selznick Lifetime Achievement Award in 2001.

Grazer grew up in the San Fernando Valley and is a graduate of the University of Southern California's School of Cinematic Arts. He began his career as a producer developing television projects. It was while producing TV pilots for Paramount Pictures in the early 1980s that Grazer first met his longtime friend and business partner Ron Howard. Their collaboration began in 1982 with the hit comedies *Night Shift* and *Splash*, and in 1986 the two founded Imagine Entertainment, which they continue to run together as chairmen.

Grazer lives in the Brentwood neighborhood of Los Angeles, and has four children. This is his first book.

Charles Fishman is an award-winning journalist and *New York Times* bestselling author. His reporting has won UCLA's Gerald Loeb Award, the highest award in business journalism, three times. His first book, *The Wal-Mart Effect*, about Wal-Mart's impact on the way Americans live, made the bestseller lists of the *New York Times* and the *Wall Street Journal*, and has become the standard for understanding Wal-Mart. His second book, *The Big Thirst*, about our conflicted relationship with water, is the bestselling book about water in a generation and is reshaping how communities approach water problems.

Fishman grew up in Miami and is a graduate of Harvard College. He started his career as a *Washington Post* reporter, and went on to work at the *Orlando Sentinel*, the *News & Observer* in Raleigh, and *Fast Company* magazine. He lives in Washington, DC, with his wife, also a journalist, and their two children.